Compulsory Winding Up Procedure

Other books by Steven A Frieze

Weaving's Notes on Bankruptcy in the County Court

Humphrey's District Registry Practice

Compulsory Winding Up Procedure

Third edition

Steven A Frieze MA (Oxon), Solicitor
*Partner in the firm of Brooke, North and Goodwin,
Leeds*

© Longman Group UK Limited 1991

ISBN 085121 7419

Published by
Longman Law, Tax and Finance
Longman Group UK Limited
21–27 Lamb's Conduit Street
London WC1N 3NJ

Associated offices
Australia, Hong Kong, Malaysia, Singapore, USA

A CIP catalogue record for this is available
from the British Library.

Printed in Great Britain by Biddles Ltd, Guildford.

Contents

Preface   ix
Table of Cases   xi
Table of Statutes   xiii
Table of Statutory Instruments   xv

1 Jurisdiction   1
  1 General matters   1
  2 The High Court   2
  3 The county courts   3
  4 Transfer between courts   3
  5 Concurrent jurisdiction   4
  6 Open court and chambers   4

2 Grounds for Winding Up   6
  1 General matters   6
  2 Inability to pay (s 122(1)(*f*))   6
  3 Just and equitable (s 122(1)(*g*))   10

3 The Winding Up Petition   13
  1 Who may petition   13
  2 Creditor's petition   14
  3 Contributories' petition   14
  4 Issue   15
  5 Service of the petition   15
  6 Verification of the petition   16
  7 Advertisement of the petition   17
  8 Advertisement as notice   18
  9 Copy petitions   18
 10 Irregularities   19

4 Interlocutory Matters   20
   1 Power to restrain the presentation, advertisement or continuance of winding up proceedings   20
   2 Power to stay or restrain other proceedings against the company   22
   3 Effect of petition on execution   22
   4 Application for the appointment of a provisional liquidator and special manager   23
   5 Avoidance of dispositions   27

5 Matters preliminary to the Hearing   28
   1 Withdrawal of the petition   28
   2 Substitution of petitioning creditor   29
   3 Certificate of compliance with the Rules   30
   4 Notice by persons who intend to appear   31
   5 List of persons who intend to appear   31
   6 Affidavits in opposition   32

6 The Hearing and the Winding Up Order   33
   1 Powers of the court on hearing the petition   33
   2 Adjournment of hearing   34
   3 Whether an order to wind up should be made   35
   4 Costs   36
   5 The order   38
   6 Rescission of the order   39
   7 Appeals   40

7 Matters arising after Winding Up   42
   1 Proceedings against the company   42
   2 Liquidator immediately after the order   42
   3 Official Receiver's duties   43
   4 Notice of the first meeting of creditors and contributories   44
   5 Rules governing meetings   44
   6 Proxies   46
   7 Business at the first meetings   48
   8 Certifying the appointment of liquidator   49
   9 Resignation of liquidator and vacancies   50
   10 Removal of liquidator   51

8 Proofs of Debt and Dividends   52
   1 Mode and form of proof   52
   2 Provable debts   53
   3 Contents of proof   53

  4 Debt payable at a future date and of a
    periodic nature   54
  5 Bills of exchange and promissory notes   54
  6 Time for proofs   54
  7 Admission and rejection of proofs   55
  8 Expunging proofs   56
  9 Interest   56
 10 VAT   57
 11 Secured creditors   57
 12 Dividends   58

9 The Liquidation Committee   60
  1 Membership and establishment of
    the committee   60
  2 Functions and rights of the Committee   61
  3 Meetings of the committee   62
  4 Resolutions by post   62
  5 Termination of membership and vacancies   63
  6 Dealings with committee members   63
  7 Expenses of members   64
  8 No committee   64

10 Rights of creditors   65

Appendix: Forms   69

Index   127

Preface

The objects of this book are twofold. One is to provide a step by step procedure for the compulsory winding up of a company registered in England and Wales including the effect of a petition for the making of an administration order. The other is to explain the procedure after a winding up order has been made. This includes the rules relating to meetings, the appointment of a liquidator and liquidation committee and proofs of debt and dividends.

Since the Insolvency Act 1986 and the Insolvency Rules 1986 only apply to post 29 December 1986 liquidations, reference should still be made to the first edition of this book for the Act and the Rules which will continue to apply to those companies whose liquidations commenced before 29 December 1986.

The interests of creditors or contributories do not cease on the making of the winding up order. It is not sufficient for a creditor or contributory simply to sit back after the winding up order has been made and trust that the right things will be done whether it be in relation to the appointment of a liquidator or the actions of the appointed liquidator. There are remedies open to a creditor or contributory. This book outlines some of these remedies where the liquidator is unwilling to act or simply dilatory in so doing.

Obviously, not every form that might be required is set out in the Appendix but the most common ones are included. These forms have been adapted from the forms set out in Schedule 4 to the Insolvency Rules 1986 and from Atkins Court Forms, volume 10 (1981 issue) to whose publishers I would like to extend my appreciation for allowing their reproduction in this book.

The Law is stated as at 14 April 1991.

Leeds
April 1991

Steven A Frieze

ix

Table of Cases

A company, *Re* [1984] 3 All ER 78 8
Bi-print Ltd, *Re*, (1982) Companies Court; 2 Insolvency Intelligence 76 ... 10
Brendacot, *Re* (1986) 2 BCC 99/164 35
Ebrahimi *v* Westbourne Galleries Ltd [1973] AC 360; [1972] 2 WLR 1289;
  116 SJ 412 11
Falcon Developments (RJ) *Re*, [1987] BCLC 437 10
Highfield Commodities Ltd *Re*, [1985] 1 WLR 149; [1984] 3 All ER 884;
  128 SJ 870 25
Hewitt Brannan Tools, *Re* (1990) BCC 354 36
Holiday Stamps Ltd, *Re* (1984) 82 LSG 2817 36
Holliday (LB) Ltd, *Re*, [1986] 2 All ER 367; [1986] PCC 330 53
Knitwear (TH) Ltd, *Re*, [1987] BCLC 86; (1986) *The Times*,
  8 November 57
Leasing and Financial Services Ltd, *Re*, (1991) BCC 29 21
Lowestoft Traffic Services Ltd, *Re*, [1986] BCLC 81 10
Lympne Investment Limited *Re*, [1972] 2 All ER 385 8
MCH Services *Re*, [1987] BCLC 535 10
Medisco Equipment Ltd, *Re* [1983] IBCC 98944; Com LR
  232 .... 9, 36, 37
Palmer Marine Survey Ltd, *Re*, [1986] 1 WLR 573; 130 SJ 372; 83 LS Gaz
  1895 .... 9, 46
Practice Direction (Solicitors: Right of Audience), May 9, 1986 [1986]
  1 WLR 545; [1986] 2 All ER 226; (1986) 83 Cr App R6 5
Practice Direction (Ch D) (Applications to Restrain Presentation of a
  Winding-Up Petition) (No 4/88) July 11, 1988 [1988] 1 WLR 988; [1988]
  2 All ER 1024 21
Practice Direction (Companies Court: Contributories' Petition) No 10,
  1990 [1990] 1 WLR 940 15
Practice Direction (Ch D) (Companies Court: Insolvency Act 1986),
  December 10, 1986 [1987] 1 WLR 53; [1987] 1 All ER 107 5
Practice Direction (Chancery Chambers), 29 July 1982 [1982] 1 WLR
  1189; [1982] 3 All ER 124 2
Practice Direction (Solicitors: Rights of Audience) [1987] All ER 107;
  [1986] 2 All ER 226 4
Rolls Razor Ltd *Re*, [1969] 3 All ER 1386 5
Stonegate Securities Ltd *v* Gregory [1980] Ch 576; [1980] 3 WLR 168;
  [1980] 1 All ER 241 CA 20

xi

Taylors Industrial Flooring *v* M & H Plant Hire *The Times*, 30 October
  1989 7
Thorpe (William) & Sons, *Re*, (1989) 5 BCC 156 10
Tompkins (HJ), *Re*, [1990] BCLC 76 10
Turner (P) (Wilsden) Ltd, *Re*, [1986] *Financial Times*, 7 November 24
Tweeds Garages Limited, *Re*, [1962] Ch 406 7
Virgo Systems Ltd, *Re*, (1989) 5 BCC 833 40
Wools (LHF) Ltd, *Re*, [1970] Ch 27; [1969] 3 WLR 100; 113 SJ 363 20
Zinotty Properties Ltd, *Re*, [1984] 3 All ER 754 9

Table of Statutes

Banking Act 1981 43
Charging Orders Act 1979 22
Companies Act 1985....................1
  ss 10, 287 15
  ss 303–304 11
  s 375................................46
  s 378................................78
  s 437................................. 6
  s 459................................14
  s 725................................. 8
  s 726............................ 8, 40
Finance Act 1991 57
Financial Services Act 1986.......... 6
Insolvency Act 1986 ....
  ....ix, 1, 2, 6, 24, 65, 75
  ss 8–27................................20
  s 10(1)(*a*), (2)(*a*), (3) 20
  s 11(1)(*a*), (3)(*c*) 20
  s 12.................................12
  s 26.................................60
  s 73................................. 6
  s 74 (2) (*f*) 53
  ss 84–116............................ 6
  s 98................................. 9
  ss 117–162 6
  s 117(2), 119(1) 3
  s 122(1)(*a*) (*f*) (*g*) 10
  s 123(*a*)..........................21, 29
    (1)(*a*) 7, 8, 21, 29, 69, 72
    (*b*) (2)........................ 7, 8
  s 124(1)..........................13, 33
    (2)................................13
    (5)............................ 9, 36
  s 125(1), (2) 33
  s 126.................................22
  s 127.................... 14, 27, 29, 34
  s 128.................................22
  s 129.................................22

Insolvency Act 1986—*contd*
    (2)............................ 1, 53
  s 130(2)...........................26, 42
  s 131.................................26
  s 132(1)..............................43
  s 133............................. 3, 66
  s 134(4), (5) 44
  s 135.................................23
  s 136, (2).............................42
    (3)................................50
    (4)............................ 41, 43
    (5), (*b*) 43
      (*c*) 43, 50
  s 137..............................43, 49
  s 139(4)..............................49
  s 140.................................13
    (1), (2), (3) 42
  s 141(5)..............................64
  s 144(1)..............................25
  s 153.................................54
  s 156.................................53
  s 164.................................48
  s 172(6)..............................50
  s 177(2)..............................25
    (4)................................99
  s 183(3)..............................22
  s 184.................................23
  s 189(2)..............................57
  s 192.................................66
  s 195......................... 7, 35, 36
  ss 212, 218 66
  ss 220–229 2
  s 221(1)(*a*) 69, 72
  s 236.................................66
  s 247(2)..............................53
  s 386..............................53, 56
  s 423.................................66
  Sched 4 ....25, 61

Insolvency Act 1986—*contd*
       para 5......................25
  Sched 6...........................53, 56
  Part 1 10
  Part II 9

Insolvency Act 1986—*contd*
  Part V 2
Protection of Depositors Act 1963
  s 6... 6

Table of Statutory Instruments

Civil Courts Order 1983 [SI No 713] 3
Companies (Winding Up) Rules 1949 [SI No 330] 1
Insolvency Fees Order 1986 [SI No 2030]
   r 9(*a*) 15
   art 11 .... 28, 36
Insolvency Rules 1986 .... ix, 1, 2, 24
   r 4.3 .... 18, 40, 55, 65
   r 4.7 13
      (2) 15, 28, 30
      (3) 15, 36
   r 4.8(3)(*a–c*) 16
   r 4.8(4), (6), (7), (9) 16
   r 4.10 16
   r 4.11 .... 17, 30
      (1), (4) 17
      (2) 16, 17
      (5) 18
   r 4.12(1), (3), (4) 17
   r 4.13 18
   r 4.14(1–3) 30
   r 4.15 28
   r 4.16(1), (2), (4), (5) 31
   r 4.17(1), (2) 31
   rr 4.17(3), 4.18 32
   r 4.19(1–3) 29
   r 4.20(1)–(3) 39
   r 4.21(1), (2)–(4) 39
   r 4.22(1), (2), (4) 14
   rr 4.23, 4.24 14
   4 4.25 23
   r 4.25(2), (3) 24
   rr 4.27, 4.28(2) 24
   rr 4.26(1), 4.28(2)
      (2) 21
   r 4.30, (4) 26
   r 4.45 67
   r 4.50 65
      (1)–(3), (5) 43
      (4) 44

r 4.52(3) 48
r 4.54(4) 47
r 4.58 49
      (2) 44
rr 4.59, 4.60(1), (2) 44
r 4.62(2) 25
r 4.63(1) 45
      (2) 49
r 4.64 46
r 4.65(4), (5) 45
r 4.67(1) (*a*) 45
          (*b*) 46
          (2) 46, 52
          (3) 45
          (4) 45
r 4.70(3) 45
      (4) 46
r 4.73, (3), (4) 52
r 4.74(2) 52
r 4.75(1), (2) 53
r 4.80(3) 66
r 4.82 55
rr 4.83, 4.86 55
    4.85 ....55, 56
rr 4.87, 4.91 54
rr 4.92(1), (2), 4.94 54
r 4.93(1), (3), (4), (6) 56
r 4.95 ....57, 58
r 4.96 57
rr 4.97(4), 4.98, 4.99 58
r 4.100(2) 49
      (4), (5) 50
r 4.108 50
      (4), (5) 50
r 4.109(2), (6) 51
rr 4.111, 4.113(3) 50
r 4.119, (2) 51
r 4.123 51
r 4.127(3) 61
r 4.150 61
          (1) 47
          (2) 48
r 4.152(3), (5) 60
r 4.153(3), (3A) 60
r 4.155(1) 61
      (2) 62
rr 4.156(1), (2), 4.157, 4.158 62
r 4.159 ....60, 62
      (2) 60
rr 4.160–1, 4.163 63
rr 4.167(1), (3), (5), 4.168 62
r 4.169 64
r 4.170(2), (3) 63

    (4) 64
rr 4.174–6 61
rr 4.180(3), 4.182(3), 4.186 59
r 4.218 .... 26, 38, 64
rr 7.11–12 3
r 7.34(1), (2) 38
r 7.47(2), (4) 40
r 7.55...19
r 7.57...52
r 7.6(2), (3), (4) 4
r 8.2(1), (2), (3)..47
r 8.6(1) 48
r 8.7 46
r 11.13 44
r 11.2(1), (1A), (2), (3)
r 11.3(1), (2) 55
r 11.5(2) 59
r 11.6(1), (2), (4) 58
r 11.7...59
r 11.11 58
r 12.3...53
r 12.4A 45
r 12.7... 1
r 12.8...61
r 12.17 66
r 13.11 18
r 67(3) 37
Sched 4 .... ix, 1, 8, 16, 17, 25, 28, 31, 39, 43, 44, 52, 69
Insolvent Partnerships Order 1986 [SI No 2142] 2
Rules of the Supreme Court 1965 [SI No 1776]—
    Ord 9, r 4(2) 16
Rules of the Supreme Court (Amendment No 2) 1982 [SI No 1111]................ 3
VAT Bad Debt Relief Regulations 1978 [SI No 1129] 57

Chapter 1

Jurisdiction

1 General Matters

This book deals with winding up proceedings of registered companies both in the High Court and in the county court.

The Act dealing with the insolvency of companies registered in England and Wales is the Insolvency Act 1986, provided that the liquidation of those companies commenced after 29 December 1986. Companies whose winding up commenced before this date are still governed by the Companies Act 1985 subject to certain transitional provisions which cause the 1986 Act to apply to these liquidations. Commencement of a winding up by the court is defined by s 129(2) as the date of presentation of the petition. In this book, references to sections are to those contained in the 1986 Act, unless otherwise stated.

The principal rules relating to winding up are the Insolvency Rules 1986 and rules referred to throughout this book are those contained in this set of rules. If the Companies Act 1985 continues to apply to the liquidation, then the Companies (Winding Up) Rules 1949 are the rules which continue to apply. See the first edition of this book for liquidations governed by the 1985 Act and 1949 Rules.

There are forms for much of the winding up procedure set out in Sched 4 to the 1986 Rules and these forms must be used with such variations, if any, as the circumstances may require (r 12.7). Many of these forms and other forms for the common situations which are likely to be encountered, are to be found in the Appendix to this book. If there is no form in Sched 4, the forms in the Appendix are suggested forms by way of precedent.

The Rules of the Supreme Court apply to winding up proceedings except where the 1986 Act or Rules stipulate something different. Similarly, the County Court Rules apply except where the 1986 Act or Rules provide otherwise.

Court Fees are prescribed by the Supreme Court Fees Orders and the County Court Fees Orders which are amended from time to time. The latest amendment was made with effect from 1 September 1990. The appropriate fees are given in the text of this book at the stage where the fees are payable except that there is a fee of £10 payable for each application to a companies court, registrar or district judge and £15 for each application to a circuit or High Court judge in each case other than applications by consent.

For the procedure regarding the winding up of unregistered companies including insolvent partnerships, see Part V of the Insolvency Act 1986 (ss 220 to 229) and the Insolvent Partnerships Order 1986.

2 The High Court

The High Court of Justice, Chancery Division has jurisdiction over all limited companies registered in England and Wales irrespective of the locality of the registered office and the amount of the authorised/issued share capital of the company. There is no 'Companies Court' distinct from the High Court. The phrase merely describes the part of the relevant division of the High Court exercising jurisdiction over companies.

Outside London, the same function as that performed by the Companies Court in London is performed by the Chancery courts with sittings at Birmingham, Bristol, Cardiff, Leeds, Liverpool, Manchester, Newcastle upon Tyne and Preston. The district registries of the High Court in these eight cities have the same jurisdiction as the Central Office in London. The district judges perform the same function as the Chancery masters and have the same powers. The Vice Chancellor of the County Palatine Court of Lancaster or his deputy sits from time to time in Leeds, Liverpool, Manchester, Newcastle upon Tyne and Preston. Chancery Division judges are allocated to sit in Birmingham, Bristol and Cardiff as and when required. These latter three cities were added to the list of those district registries with Chancery and hence companies' jurisdiction by SI 1982 No 1111 and a *Practice Direction*, 29 July 1982 ([1982] 3 All ER 124). Each of the eight cities referred to above has unlimited jurisdiction in winding up proceedings and are not confined to companies whose registered offices are situated within the circuit in which the particular registry is situated.

3 The county courts

Where a company has a paid up share capital not exceeding £120,000 and its registered office is situated within the district of a particular county court, then that court has jurisdiction over the winding up of that company in exactly the same way as the High Court (s 117(2)). Not all county courts have this jurisdiction. Basically, it is those county courts which have jurisdiction in bankruptcy which also have jurisdiction to entertain winding up proceedings. The Metropolitan county courts have no jurisdiction in bankruptcy and accordingly have no jurisdiction in winding up. These courts are attached to the High Court for the purposes of winding up and bankruptcy. The Civil Courts Order 1983 as amended, specifies which county courts have such jurisdiction. A list appears in the *County Court Practice* (the Green Book) each year.

4 Transfer between courts

At any time, either with or without the application of the parties, any proceedings relating to the winding up of a company may be transferred from one court to another (r 7.11). Where proceedings are commenced in the wrong court, the court may transfer the proceedings, allow them to continue where they are or strike them out (r 7.12). It is possible for certain questions arising in winding up proceedings in a county court to be determined by a High Court judge in the form of a special case (s 119(1)).

5 Concurrent jurisdiction

It must be noted that as a result of the overlapping jurisdiction of the High Court sitting in London and the eight provincial cities referred to above and the county court for the district in which the registered office of the company is situated, proceedings to wind up a company could be commenced in as many as ten different courts. Care must be taken, particularly in relation to searches for prior creditors' petitions for the compulsory winding up of a company, that action has not already been commenced in another court. Once a winding up petition has been advertised, this is regarded as notice to the world and any petition issued subsequent to the date of advertisement is likely to be dismissed with no order for costs if a winding up order is, or has been, made on a prior petition.

Enquiries can be made of the Central Index of Winding Up petitions at the Companies Court in London by telephoning 071 430 0630. Wherever a petition has been issued, it will be noted in this index. The service is free of charge.

6 Open court and chambers

Unless specified otherwise, all applications in the course of proceedings to wind up a company are heard in chambers. In the High Court, petitions, applications for committal and examinations under s 133 (public examination of directors or other officers) are dealt with in open court. In the county court, similar rules apply.

Unless a circuit or High Court judge has given a general or special direction to the contrary or the order sought is not within the district judge's or companies court registrar's power to make, every application must first be made to a registrar (High Court) or district judge (r 7.6(2)). The registrar may adjourn any matter to a judge (r 7.6(3)). Nothing in the Rules precludes an application being made directly to a judge in a proper case (r 7.6(4)).

By virtue of a *Practice Direction* dated December 10 1986 ([1987] All ER 107) winding up petitions and most other forms of petition will be heard by the registrar of the Companies Court in London, rather than by a High Court judge, and solicitors, properly robed, have the right of audience before the registrar sitting in open court as a result of a *Practice Direction* dated May 9 1986 ([1986] 2 All ER 226). The *Practice Direction* dated 10 December 1986 also provides that various applications, such as to extend or abridge time, to withdraw petitions, for the substitution of a petitioner and for leave for a liquidator to resign will be dealt with by the Chief Clerk of the Companies Court. In the county court and the eight provincial district registries with Chancery jurisdiction, petitions are heard by a district judge in open court.

Appeals against an *ex parte* order of a district judge can be made by notice of motion to the judge seeking the discharge or variation of the order. See, eg, *Re Rolls Razor Ltd* [1969] 3 All ER 1386.

Chapter 2

Grounds for Winding Up

1 General matters

There are two modes of winding up provided for in s 73:
- (a) by the court (or compulsory winding up) (ss 84–116); and
- (b) voluntary (either creditors' or members') (ss 117–162).

A company may be wound up by the court if:
- (a) it has resolved by special resolution that it should be so wound up (s 122(1)(a)), or
- (b) it is unable to pay its debts (s 122(1)(f)), or
- (c) the court is of the opinion that it is just and equitable that it should be wound up (s 122(1)(g)).

There are a number of other grounds entitling the court to make a winding up order but those set out above are the grounds most common and most appropriate when considering the position of creditors of a company or the company itself. The Secretary of State can petition if it appears to him to be expedient in the public interest as a result of a report from inspectors appointed under s 437 of the Companies Act 1985. He also has special powers to apply for the winding up of a company to which s 6 of the Protection of Depositors Act 1963 applies and under the Financial Services Act 1986.

2 Inability to pay (s 122(1)(f))

A creditor who is unable to obtain payment from a company of monies due to him is entitled as of right to a winding up order if he petitions the court and brings his case within the Act. He

6

is not bound to allow the company time to pay nor is he bound to accept a voluntary winding up once the debt is established and remains unsatisfied. It is not a discretionary matter. It is no defence for the company to say that there are no assets or that a debenture holder as a secured creditor will take all that there is. Regard, however, may be had for the wishes of other creditors (s 195). See Chapter 6 below for the principles on which a winding up order will be made when there is opposition from other creditors or shareholders.

A winding up order will not be made where the creditor's debt is not beyond dispute. A winding up petition is not a legitimate means of enforcing payment of a debt which is *bona fide* in dispute. The practice of standing over petitions on disputed debts until the dispute is resolved is no longer followed unless there is reason to believe that once established as due, the debt will not be paid. See also Chapter 4 on the power of the court to restrain winding up proceedings.

If liability for a debt is admitted but the quantum is in dispute, a winding up order may be made (*Re Tweeds Garages Limited* [1962] Ch 406) but if there is a counterclaim equal to or greater than the claim, the usual practice is to dismiss or stay the petition.

There are three alternative situations where a company is deemed unable to pay its debts. First, if a creditor (by assignment or otherwise) who is owed more than £750 has, by leaving it at its registered office, served on the company a statutory demand requiring the company to pay the sum owing and the company has for three weeks thereafter neglected to pay (s 123(1)(*a*)). Second, if execution on a judgment is returned unsatisfied in whole or in part (s 123(1)(*b*)). Third, if it is proved to the satisfaction of the court that the company is unable to pay its debts, including contingent and prospective liabilities (s 123(2)). Even in the absence of an unsatisfied execution, there is no requirement that a petitioner must have served a statutory demand. If a debt was due and unpaid and could not be disputed on some substantial ground, that was of itself evidence of inability to pay (*Taylors Industrial Flooring v M & H Plant Hire* (*The Times*, 30 October 1989)).

If the exact amount owed by the company to the creditor is not known and is indeed in dispute, the creditor is not in a position to serve a statutory demand even if the company had offered to pay part of the debt and neglected to do so (*Re a Company* [1984] 3 All ER 78).

Where two or more creditors combine who are each owed less than £750 but together are owed more than £750, it is thought that they are entitled to a winding up order, having served the appropriate demand under s 123(1)(*a*). For the form of statutory demand under s 123(1)(*a*) set out in Sched 4 to the Rules (form 4.1), see the Appendix, Form 1. The demand under s 123(1)(*a*) must be signed by or on behalf of the creditor. The demand must be left at the registered office of the company. It is also questionable whether service by post on the company at its registered office complies with the section. Documents may be served on a company by leaving them or sending them by post to the registered office of the company (s 725 of the Companies Act 1985) but in s 123(1)(*a*) the alternative is not given.

Payment must be made and received by the creditor within 21 days if a petition is to be defended. Twenty-one clear days must be allowed (*Re Lympne Investment Limited* [1972] 2 All ER 385). Effectively, therefore, a notice served on 1 February should not found a petition issued earlier than 23 February.

The fact that the sheriff is in possession of the company's assets will not be sufficient to found a petition under s 123(1)(*b*) but it may be under s 123(2). Only if the sheriff has made a *nulla bona* return or a partial return will such return be available to an unsatisfied creditor (s 123(1)(*b*).

Inability to pay debts is judged according to the commercial definition of insolvency, that is, inability to meet debts as they fall due (the 'cash flow test'). It is not enough to say that the company has sufficient assets to ensure that all its creditors will be paid in full ultimately. A company may be both wealthy (in terms of assets) and insolvent (because it has no cash available to meet immediate debts due).

Winding up will also be ordered (as s 123(2) envisages) in another kind of insolvency, that is, if the assets of the company present and future will be insufficient to meet all of its liabilities, actual, contingent and prospective (the 'balance sheet test').

The mere fact that an administrative receiver has been appointed by a secured creditor does not automatically mean that a company is unable to pay its debts (compare with cases under s 726 of the Companies Act 1985 where security for costs can be ordered against a company of doubtful means wishing to pursue litigation) but it is strong evidence of the company's inability to pay debts unless a statement of affairs has been lodged showing a likely surplus of assets for both secured and unsecured creditors. Likewise with a petition for the appointment of an administrator under Part II of the Act. However, in the latter case, any winding up proceedings as with other forms of proceedings against the company, are automatically stayed pending the hearing of the petition and even afterwards if an administration order is made. For more details of the effect of a petition for an administration order, see Chapter 4.

Where a creditor has a judgment against the company, a winding up petition may be ordered to stand over upon the company's undertaking to apply to have the judgment set aside where there appears to be a reasonable prospect of the application being successful. A winding up order will not be refused if a judgment is under appeal unless a stay of execution has also been granted.

If a company has given notice to its creditors under the provisions of s 98 (creditors' voluntary winding up), this is *prima facie* evidence of inability to pay debts since the company's shareholders are proposing to pass a resolution to wind up the company because the company cannot by reason of its liabilities continue to trade.

But where the company is already in voluntary liquidation, a winding up order will not be made unless the court is satisfied that the voluntary liquidation cannot be continued with due regard to the interests of the company's creditors and contributories (s 124(5)). This applies where the winding up petition was not presented until after the voluntary liquidation had begun and follows the view expressed in *Re Medisco Equipment Ltd* (1983) 1 BCC 98944. However, the position would be different if the petition was issued prior to the meeting of contributories and creditors to place the company into creditors' voluntary liquidation since in the event of a winding up order being made by the court, the commencement of the liquidation would be deemed to be from an earlier date thus giving rise to the right to challenge action of the former officers of the companies further back in time.

It was held in *Re Zinotty Properties Ltd* [1984] 3 All ER 754 that the failure to hold a properly quorate contributories' meeting to resolve to wind up was sufficient to justify a winding up order made to supersede a voluntary winding up. It was held in *Re Palmer Marine Survey Ltd* [1986] 1 WLR 673 that, because of the way in which the creditor's nominee as liquidator was defeated (by the director/chairman utilising the votes of ten small creditors which he controlled) the proper course was for a winding up order to be made. In *Re Lowestoft Traffic Services Ltd* [1986] BCLC 81 the desire that the creditors should have confidence in the liquidator's independence and the circumstances of the liquidator's appointment causing the creditors disquiet were enough to justify the making of a winding up order. The possibility of a conflict of interest that the voluntary liquidator might be faced with has also been held sufficient to warrant the making of a winding up order after vountary liquidation where the views of opposing and supporting creditors cancelled each other out (see eg, *Re Bi-print Ltd* 1982, Companies Court (2 Insolvency Intelligence 76)). There are other cases decided under both the old law and the Insolvency Act dealing with the 'conversion' of voluntary liquidations into compulsory liquidations, eg, *R J Falcon Developments* [1987] BCLC 437, *MCH Services* [1987] BCLC 535, *Re William Thorpe & Sons* (1989) 5 BCC 156 and *H J Tompkins* [1990] BCLC 76.

The mere fact that a company has written to its creditors proposing that it should discharge its obligations to its creditors by instalments or at a date in the future (that is, a moratorium) or proposes a voluntary arrangement with its creditors under Part I of the Act is also *prima facie* evidence of inability to pay debts as they have fallen due, that is, insolvency.

3 Just and equitable (s 122(1)(*g*))

A contributory, that is, a shareholder or member, may petition the court to wind up a company under the just and equitable doctrine, but there must be strong grounds for making a winding up order at the instance of a contributory. In deciding whether or not to make a winding up order, the court exercises a judicial discretion. If there are no obstacles in the way of a voluntary winding up, the court may refuse to make a winding up order. The petition of the administrator or supervisor is treated as a contributory's petition. But where the directors of a company had no *bona fide* intentions to carry on the business properly or where there are matters to be investigated and there was overwhelming influence being exercised by one director, an order will be made.

The following are some of the heads under which the court will exercise its discretion to order winding up under the just and equitable doctrine:

(1) substratum gone—eg, where a company has no reasonable prospect of carrying out a contract which its main object was to carry out, a winding up order will be made;

(2) deadlock or disagreement in the management—cases relating to partnerships have been applied by analogy (eg, *Ebrahimi v Westbourne Galleries Limited* [1973] AC 360). Equity is to prevail. Thus if a petitioner can show that the circumstances are such that it would be inequitable to allow legal rights to be made use of to the prejudice of others, eg, the right to remove a director under ss 303, and 304 of the Companies Act 1985, then a winding up order may be made. Legal rights are subjected to equitable considerations. Examples of such situations may include:

(*a*) problems caused by loss of confidence in personal relationship between the shareholders—typically in the case of a company carrying on business formerly operated by the shareholders in partnership,

(*b*) the rights of sleeping partners,

(*c*) the restriction upon transfer of shares so that when one shareholder ceases to be involved in the management of the company, he is unable to dispose of his shares on proper terms.

Because equitable principles apply, the petitioner himself must come with clean hands and must not be the one who caused the situation to arise leading to the breakdown of personal relationship or mutual confidence;

(3) fraud or illegality—where a company has been initiated or is being carried on fraudulently and where the controlling shareholders are implicated in the fraud and a winding up order is necessary to ensure that a proper investigation is carried out or to facilitate the recovery of improper profits or is the only way to end the fraudulent business, a winding up order will be made;

(4) mismanagement or misapplication of funds—eg, where a company is so constituted that it is deprived of its usual remedies for mismanagement or misapplication of funds by reason of the defaulters being in control, a winding up order will be made;

(5) a bubble company—if a company never had a proper foun-

dation, eg, in the pyramid or franchise cases, it is just and equitable that it should be wound up.

Chapter 3

The Winding Up Petition

1 Who may petition

An application to the court to wind up a company must be by way of petition (s 124(1)).

The company itself, any creditor or creditors (including any contingent or prospective creditor) or any contributory or contributories, together or separately, may petition for the winding up of a company, except that a contributory will not be entitled to present a winding up petition unless either the number of contributories has fallen below two (in the case of a private company or seven in any other case), or he has held shares in the company for at least six months during the 18 months prior to petitioning (s 124(2)).

The company acting through the agency of its directors can present a petition without the authority of a general meeting of contributories. The resolution of the directors has been held sufficient and the petition should state the fact that the directors have so resolved. An administrative receiver can petition as can an administrator or a supervisor but if the administrator or supervisor wishes to be appointed liquidator under s 140, he must say so in the petition, tell creditors and report to the court what creditors have said in response (r 4.7).

For the effect of the provisions of the administration procedure on winding up petitions, see Chapter 4, section 1.

2 Creditor's petition

A creditor in equity as well as a creditor in law may petition. The assignee of a debt can petition, including an equitable assignee. A garnishor of debt due from a company is, however, not a creditor. He merely holds a charge over the debt due to the garnishee. There is no reason why a secured creditor cannot petition (without first realising his security) for the shortfall on his security having valued the same, though normally such a creditor would rely first of all on his security and petition for the shortfall when ascertained.

There is a form of petition in Sched 4 to the Rules (form 4.2). For this form of petition, see the Appendix, Form 3 and variations to the standard form, Forms 4 to 10.

3 Contributories' petition

A contributories' petition must specify the grounds upon which it is presented and the nature of the relief sought (r 4.22(1)). There is a contributory's petition set out in Sched 4 to the Rules (form 4.14), see the Appendix, Form 11. On presentation of a contributories' petition, the court does not fix a date for the hearing of the petition but a return day when the registrar or district judge will give directions for the prosecution of the petition (r 4.22(2)). The petition must be served at least 14 days before the return day (r 4.22(4)). The directions which the court can give relate to the persons to be served, the venue of the hearing, advertisement of the petition, the manner in which evidence is to be adduced and whether particulars of claim and defence are to be delivered (r 4.23). Otherwise the procedure as to notice of appearance and list of appearances etc follows the procedure for creditors' petitions (r 4.24). It is not necessary for a contributory's petition under the Companies Act 1985, s 459 (unfair prejudice) to include, automatically, a prayer for the winding up of the company. It should only be included where the petitioner prefers such a remedy. If it is included, the petitioner should also state if he consents or objects to an order under s 127 in standard form permitting dispositions of the company's property pending the hearing (*Practice Direction (Companies Court: Contributories' Petition) (No 10 1990)* [1990] 1 WLR 940).

4 Issue

Petitions can be issued in the High Court either in the Central Office or in the district registries at Birmingham, Bristol, Cardiff, Leeds, Liverpool, Manchester, Newcastle upon Tyne and Preston, wherever the registered office of the company is situated, and in the county court having jurisdiction in bankruptcy for the district in which the registered office of the company is situated provided that the issued share capital of the company does not exceed £120,000. For jurisdiction generally, see Chapter 1.

Requirements on issue:

(*a*) petition and three copies on A4 size paper (photocopies, not carbon copies) plus a copy for any voluntary liquidator, administrator or supervisor of voluntary arrangement (r 4.7(3));

(*b*) fee (£40);

(*c*) receipt for the deposit payable (r 4.7(2)), namely, £270 (Insolvency Fees Order 1986 as amended r 9(*a*));

(*d*) if by post, addressed envelope.

The endorsement as to the date, time and place of hearing will be completed before the petition is sealed. All copies of the petition will be sealed and handed back. One sealed copy of the petition is required for service, one for exhibiting to the affidavit of service, one for exhibiting to the affidavit verifying the petition (the copy usually stamped 'Filed', that is, the court's copy) and one for retention by the petitioner's solicitor. Additional sealed copies are required for service if there is already a voluntary liquidator, administrator or supervisor of voluntary arrangement.

5 Service of the petition

Every petition must, unless presented by the company itself, be served on the company at its registered office (as last notified to the registrar of companies under the Companies Act 1985, s 10 or s 287) of if there is no registered office, at its principal or last known place of business, by leaving a copy with any director or other officer or employee of the company there (r 4.8(3)(*a*)) or with any person who acknowledges himself to be authorised to accept service (r 4.8(3)(*b*)). If there is no such person to be found there, it is served by depositing it at or about the registered office in such a way that it is likely to come to the notice of a person attending the office (r 4.8(3)(*c*)). If the company is already in voluntary liquidation, administration, receivership or under a voluntary arrangement, the petition must also be served on the relevant insolvency practitioner on the next business day after the company was served (r 4.10).

Service of the petition must be effected at least 14 days before the hearing date. RSC Ord 9, r 4(2) requires service to be effected not less than seven days before the hearing date. However, r 4.11(2) (advertisement of the petition) requires that advertisement of the petition is not to be made until seven days after service on the company. These two requirements taken together mean that at least 14 days must elapse between service of the petition on the company and the hearing date. From a practical point of view and since it is difficult to predict the edition of the *London Gazette* in which the advertisement will appear, care should be taken to serve the petition well in advance of 14 days before the hearing date.

If for any reason service of the petition at the registered office is not practicable, service at some other place in England and Wales at which the company carried on business or by delivering it to the secretary, or some director, manager or principal officer of the company wherever that person may be found in such a way that it is likely to come to the attention of a person attending there (r 4.8(4)) or the court may, on application, order service in some other way (r 4.8(6) and (7)).

Service must be proved by affidavit specifying the manner of service (r 4.9). There are affidavits of service in Sched 4 to the Rules: form 4.4 (service at registered office) and form 4.5 (service other than at registered office): see the Appendix, Forms 13 and 14.

6 Verification of the petition

Every petition must be verified by an affidavit that the statements in the petition are true to the best of the deponent's belief (r 4.12(1)). Schedule 4 to the Rules contains such an affidavit (form 4.3), see the Appendix, Form 12. The affidavit must be made by the petitioner, or by one of the petitioners if more than one, or by some person, such as a director, company secretary or similar officer of the petitioning creditor or a solicitor who has been concerned in the matter on behalf of the petitioner or by some responsible person who is duly authorised and who has the requisite knowledge (r 4.12(4)). A more detailed affidavit will be required for petitions by contributories who claim that they have been unfairly prejudiced by the company.

There is now no time limit for filing this affidavit though r 4.11 suggests that the affidavit must be lodged at the same time as the petition itself and the registrar's certificate of compliance with the Rules (see Chapter 5, section 3) will not be issued if the affidavit verifying the petition has not yet been filed.

The affidavit must exhibit a sealed copy of the petition (r 4.12(3)).

7 Advertisement of the petition

Unless the court otherwise directs, every petition must be advertised once in the *London Gazette* not less than seven business days after it has been served on the company and not less than seven business days before the day fixed for the hearing (r 4.11(1) and (2)). The advertisement must state the name and registered office of the company, the name and address (or registered office) of the petitioner, the date of presentation of the petition, the venue of the hearing, the name and address of the petitioner's solicitors and that any person intending to support or oppose the petition must give notice of his intention (r 4.11(4)). Schedule 4 to the Rules contains the form of advertisement (form 4.6), see the Appendix, Form 15.

It is no longer necessary to advertise a petition in a local newspaper though such advertisement is still sometimes made when it is desired to obtain support for a petition to which opposition from the company and/or some other creditors is anticipated.

The form of advertisement should be sent either to an advertising agent or direct to the offices of the *London Gazette*, HMSO Publications Centre, 51 Nine Elms Lane, London SW8 5DR (tel: 071–873 8300) together with a cheque for the fee of £21.23 which includes VAT and the cost of one copy of the *Gazette*. Copies of the *Gazette* can also be obtained via HMSO.

The court has a discretion under r 4.3 to extend or abridge time limits and this applies to the time for advertisement as well.

If the petition cannot be heard on the date fixed for hearing because the advertisement has not appeared sufficiently in advance, the petition may be dismissed (r 4.11(5)) or stood over with liberty to readvertise. The costs of the readvertisement may not be allowed unless the fault is not that of the petitioner. There were many cases in the nineteenth century dealing with the problems of defective advertisement including the absence from the advertisement of certain information, such as the footnote relating to support or opposition to the petition. Whilst in some cases the irregularities were waived, in others they were not and only strict compliance with the rules can avoid difficulty.

8 Advertisement as notice

Advertisement of the petition is notice to all the world of its presentation. If a second petition is issued after the first petition has been advertised, the second petition would be liable to be dismissed and that petitioner have no order for costs in his favour. With the facility of the Central Index of Winding Up Petitions at the Companies Court in London available free of charge by simply telephoning 071–430 0630, there is no excuse for a second petition being issued even if the first petition had not then been advertised unless both petitions were issued within a day or so of each other and in different courts.

9 Copy petitions

Every director, contributory or creditor is entitled to a copy of the petition from the petitioner or his solicitor within two days of requiring the same on payment of the appropriate fee for such copy, currently 15p per sheet (r 4.13 and r 13.11).

10 Irregularities

No proceedings will be invalidated by any formal defect or any irregularity unless the court considers that substantial injustice has been caused by it and that the injustice cannot be remedied by an order of the court (r 7.55). A statutory demand is not a proceeding under the Act or Rules and so is not covered by r 7.55.

Chapter 4

Interlocutory Matters

1 Power to restrain the presentation, advertisement or continuance of winding up proceedings

The effect of the administration provisions in ss 8 to 27 on winding up petitions can be summarised as follows:

(a) after the presentation of a petition for the appointment of an administrator, no winding up order can be made (s 10(1)(a)) unless an administrative receiver has already been appointed and he does not consent to the making of an administration order (s 10(3));

(b) however, the presentation of such a petition does not preclude the presentation of a winding up petition (s 10(2)(a));

(c) if the petition for an administration order is dismissed or withdrawn, a winding up order on the pending winding up petition can subsequently be made (s 10(1)(a));

(d) if an administration order is made any winding up petition must be dismissed (s 11(1)(a));

(e) no winding up petition can be presented after an administration order has been made except with the leave of the court or the administrator (s 11(3)(c)).

A winding up petition is not a legitimate means of seeking to enforce payment of a debt which is genuinely in dispute (see Chapter 2, section 2). If a debt is not disputed but the company has a genuine cross claim or set off against the petitioner which, if established, would extinguish the liability, the petition may be stayed (*Re LHF Wools Ltd* [1970] Ch 27).

An injunction to restrain the presentation of a winding up petition by an unreasonable creditor whose claim was genuinely in dispute should be granted without any condition as to the swearing of a declaration of solvency by the company being imposed (*Stonegate Securities Ltd v Gregory* [1980] 1 All ER 241). Such a situation may come about where a creditor serves a statutory demand under s 123(1)(*a*) on the company in relation to a disputed debt, thereby indicating his intention to petition if his debt is not paid within the time limited by the section. But presentation of a petition will not be restrained even where the petitioner had previously commenced High Court proceedings which had yet to result in a judgment (*Re Leasing and Financial Services* [1991] BCC 29).

If a petition is not presented *bona fide* and for the legitimate purpose of obtaining a winding up order, the court will restrain the advertisement of the petition and stay all further proceedings upon it. An application to stay advertisement is made in the winding up proceedings and must be made by originating motion to the Companies Court or one of the eight provincial district registries with chancery jurisdiction (*Practice Direction* 11 July 1988). The automatic delay between service and advertisement gives the company the opportunity to make the necessary application.

The motion should be supported by an affidavit setting out the grounds upon which the application is made. Two clear days' notice must be given but in urgent cases an *ex parte* application could be made.

For a precedent of the notice of motion and orders, see the Appendix Forms 16, 17 and 18.

Requirements on issue:

(*a*) motion and copy (not carbon),

(*b*) affidavit in support, and

(*c*) fee of £15.

Upon the hearing of the motion, if the court is of the view that there is a genuine dispute as to the petitioner's debt or there is some other reason rendering it certain that a winding up order will not be made, it can order that the petitioner be restrained from advertising the petition. Since it is not possible to obtain a winding up order on a petition that has not been advertised, this has the same effect as dismissing the petition. If, however, the order restraining advertisement is only until some act is done by either party or some event occurs, then merely staying advertisement and allowing the petition itself to stand over may be of use since eventually the petition may be proceeded with and then priority as to the date of commencement of winding up will be preserved.

2 Power to stay or restrain other proceedings against the company

At any time after the presentation of a winding up petition (and before a winding up order is made) the company itself or any creditor or contributory may apply to the court for a stay of any other proceedings against the company. The application is made in the winding up proceedings unless the proceedings sought to be stayed are proceedings in the High Court (s 126). The court can stay the proceedings on such terms as it thinks fit.

The application to stay is made *ex parte* on motion, the applicant giving the usual undertakings as to damages. The stay applies until after the petition has been disposed of.

3 Effect of petition on execution

Execution is a proceeding in the action and can be stayed by application to the court which granted the judgment which it is sought to execute. Where a company is being wound up by the court, any attachment, sequestration, distress or execution put in force against the company after the commencement of the winding up (the commencement of the winding up is deemed by s 129 to be the presentation of a petition provided a winding up is subsequently made on the petition) shall be void for all purposes (s 128).

If execution is issued and the sheriff is actually in possession before a petition is presented, an order restraining the judgment creditor from proceeding with the execution would not normally be made. However, if a winding up order is made before the execution is complete, the creditor will not be allowed to keep the benefit of his execution. An execution is complete when either goods seized are sold, or if a charging order is made under the Charging Orders Act 1979 or, an attachment of debt having been made by way of a garnishee order, the debt has been received (s 183(3)). If monies are paid to the sheriff to avoid a sale, he must retain them for 14 days and if during that time the sheriff receives notice of the presentation of a winding up petition, the sheriff cannot account to the execution creditor but must hold them until after the petition has been disposed of. He will then either pay the monies to the liquidator or, if no winding up order is made, to the execution creditor.

If execution is issued after the presentation of a winding up petition or if execution is issued before but the sheriff does not gain possession until after the presentation of the petition, further action by the sheriff will be stayed on application by the company in the absence of special circumstances in favour of the execution creditor (s 184).

The rules relating to distress are slightly different. If distress is levied before the presentation of a winding up petition but is not completed by sale until after, the court could, but would not normally, restrain the sale or stop the creditor levying distress of the benefit.

4 Application for the appointment of a provisional liquidator and special manager

After a petition for the winding up by the court of a company has been presented upon the application of a creditor, a contributory or the company itself, and upon proof by affidavit of sufficient ground for the appointment of a provisional liquidator, the court, if it thinks fit and upon such terms as in the opinion of the court are just and necessary, may appoint a provisional liquidator (s 135 and r 4.25). For a provisional liquidator to be appointed, it is necessary for the applicant to show that assets of the company are somehow in jeopardy and unless a provisional liquidator is appointed, there is a real fear that the assets of the company will not be available for distribution amongst creditors in the proper way once a winding up order has been made and a liquidator appointed. It is necessary to allege that some wrongdoing is being perpetrated against the company which cannot be remedied by action by the ultimate liquidator against the wrongdoer.

The affidavit in support must also state whether to the applicant's knowledge the company has proposed or there is in force a voluntary arrangement, an administrator, administrative receiver or voluntary liquidator has been appointed, if it is pro-

posed that someone other than the Official Receiver be provisional liquidator, has that person consented and is he a qualified insolvency practitioner, and whether the Official Receiver
has been informed of the application and given a copy of it and
an estimate of the value of the company's assets (r 4.25(2)). The
Official Receiver must be given a copy of the affidavit and
informed of the hearing of the application so that he can attend
and make representations. If it is not practicable to comply with
this requirement, the Official Receiver must be informed of the
application in sufficient time to enable him to attend (r 4.25(3)).

An order appointing a provisional liquidator has been refused
where the company is already in voluntary liquidation and the
object of the petition was to replace the voluntary liquidator with
another liquidator of the creditors' choosing. The court expressed
the view that since the normal function of a provisional liquidator
was merely to gather in and preserve the assets and records of
the company until the hearing of the petition, there was little
purpose in replacing the liquidator already in position whose
duty it was to do at least the same. However, where the voluntary
liquidator cannot see the conflict of interest he faces due to his
role as liquidator of an associated company, he may be displaced
by a provisional liquidator after the presentation of a winding
up petition (*Re P Turner (Wilsden) Ltd* (1986) *Financial Times*,
7 November).

Before an order appointing the Official Receiver as provisional
liquidator can be issued, the applicant is required to lodge with
the Official Receiver a deposit against the Official Receiver's
remuneration and expenses for acting as provisional liquidator
(r 4.27). If someone other than the Official Receiver is appointed
provisional liquidator, the Rules provide that the cost of provid-
ing the security required of him under the Act will be, in the
first instance, payable by him subject to reimbursement out of
the company's assets (r 4.28(2)). However, there is no mention
in the Act of the requirement to provide a separate security when
acting as provisional liquidator so presumably the reimbursement
relates to a proportion of the cost of the qualified insolvency
practitioner's overall security required by the various professional
bodies who are authorised to issue insolvency practitioner
licences.

For a precedent of the provisional liquidator's consent to act,
see the Appendix, Form 23. The application to appoint a provisional liquidator is made by summons to the registrar or district

judge for the court in which the winding up petition was presented. The company is made the respondent unless, of course, the company is itself the applicant for the appointment. For the form of summons and precedent of the affidavit in support, see the Appendix, Forms 19 and 20.

In urgent cases the application can be made *ex parte*. In such cases the applicant will normally be required to give an undertaking as to damages. See, eg, *Re Highfield Commodities Ltd* [1984] 3 All ER 884.

The order appointing the provisional liquidator must state the nature and functions to be carried out by the provisional liquidator (r 4.26(1)). There is a form of such order in Sched 4 to the Rules (form 4.15), see the Appendix, Form 21. For precedents of the types of powers that the provisional liquidator might be given, see the Appendix, Form 22.

A provisional liquidator does not have the power to trade without sanction (para 5 of Sched 4 to the Act). If the company is still trading, it is desirable that the provisional liquidator be given sanction to continue trading or for a special management to be appointed under s 177. Where the Official Receiver is appointed provisional liquidator and it is desirable that the company continue trading, he may seek to appoint another person as special manager to carry on the trading.

The application for the appointment of a special manager may be made by the provisional liquidator where it appears to him that the nature of the business or the property of the company or the interests of the creditors or contributories require the appointment of another person to manage the company's business or property (s 177(2)). A special manager does not have to be a qualified insolvency practitioner but is required to give security calculated by reference to the value of the company's assets. There is a form of order appointing a special manager in Sched 4 to the Rules (form 4.60), see the Appendix, Form 24.

The registrar or district judge gives notice of the order to the Official Receiver (r 4.62(2)). Whenever a provisional liquidator has been appointed, he must take into his custody or under his control all the property and things in action to which the company appears to be entitled (s 144(1)). The powers of a liquidator set out in Sched 4 to the Act are not specifically given to a provisional liquidator and therefore the provisional liquidator's powers are only those which are given to him by the order appointing him. As a provisional liquidator does not have a liquidation committee, he will only be able to exercise some of these powers with the sanction of the court.

It sometimes happens that the company, a contributory or creditor is unhappy with the extent of the powers of the provisional liquidator. He can apply to the court for the provisional liquidator's powers to be restricted or further defined and the provisional liquidator can, of course, apply to the court for directions. Such an application is made to the registrar or district judge on summons. In urgent cases, an *ex parte* application can be made.

If a winding up order is made, the appointment of the provisional liquidator automatically ceases and the Official Receiver becomes the liquidator until a meeting of creditors takes place (assuming that the Official Receiver resolves that one should be summoned) and some person is appointed liquidator, whether this is the Official Receiver or someone else. The provisional liquidator's fees are payable out of the assets of the company in the prescribed order of priority (r 4.218).

If no winding up order is made on the petition or if the petition is stayed or dismissed, the appointment of the provisional liquidator comes to an end but the provisional liquidator is entitled to be paid, out of the assets of the company, those fees fixed by the court having regard to the time he and his staff have spent, the value and nature of the assets, the complexity of the matter etc and may retain the company's assets to meet those costs (r 4.30).

Under s 131, within 21 days of the appointment of a provisional liquidator (as well as on the appointment of a permanent liquidator) the directors are required to furnish the Official Receiver with a statement of the company's affairs in the prescribed form (form 4.17). Such a statement should be available before the hearing of the petition. If the Official Receiver takes steps for the purpose of obtaining such a statement of affairs or has performed any other duty, he can look to the provisional liquidator for the payment of a fee (r 4.30(4)).

When a provisional liquidator has been appointed (as when a winding up order has been made) no proceedings may be commenced or continued against the company except with leave of the court (s 130(2)).

5 Avoidance of dispositions

Under s 127, in a winding up by the court, any disposition of the property of the company, including things in action and any transfer of shares or alteration in the status of the members of the company, made after the commencement of the winding up, is void unless the court otherwise orders.

The section thus prevents any improper dissipation of the company's assets being effective from the date of presentation of the winding up petition, assuming that a winding up order is made on that petition ultimately. The section also has the effect of paralysing the trade of the company for no-one can deal safely with the company for fear of their transactions being subsequently set aside. The section gives the court discretion to validate, either retrospectively or in advance, any transaction which the company proposes to enter into.

The company can apply to the court on a motion for an order that a particular disposition of the property of the company, eg, the sale of a piece of property or the continued operation by the company of its bank account, will not be made void pursuant to s 127 in the event of a winding up order being made on the hearing of the petition. The petitioner will be made the respondent to the motion and can appear at the hearing. The order made on the motion will specify those transactions which the company can enter into.

It is unlikely that an order would be made if its effect was to give some form of preference to any individual creditor. The object of the procedure is to enable the company to trade during the pendency of the proceedings and consent would normally only be given to enter into transactions at arm's length values or for the payment to creditors for goods to be purchased.

Chapter 5

Matters preliminary to the Hearing

1 Withdrawal of the petition

When the petitioning creditor has been paid his debt or does not wish for some other reason to proceed with his petition, the petition should be withdrawn. If the petition has not yet been served, then the petitioner lodges with the court a request to withdraw the petition duly signed on his behalf. The registrar or district judge will then give leave for the petition to be withdrawn. If the petition has already been served, leave to withdraw the petition must be obtained. If at least five days before the hearing the petitioner, on an *ex parte* application, satisfies the court that the petition has not been advertised, no notices of support or opposition to the petition have been received and the company consents, then leave may be granted (r 4.15). For the form of order giving leave to withdraw, see the Apendix, Form 25 (form 4.8 in Sched 4 to the Rules). If the winding up petition is withdrawn, the petitioner is entitled to the return of the deposit paid on issue under r 4.7(2) (Insolvency Fees Order 1986, art, r 11).

Once the petition has been advertised, any application to withdraw must be made on the hearing of the petition. The reason for this is that some other creditor, who, unlike the petitioning creditor, has not been paid his debt, may wish to be substituted as petitioning creditor. If there is no one wishing to take over the conduct of the proceedings, then the usual order is for the petition to be dismissed, not for leave to withdraw to be given.

A cautious petitioner will, however, be very reluctant to agree to his petition being withdrawn without being reasonably certain that no other creditor will take over his petition, for, having

28

agreed to drop out of the proceedings because he has been paid, he may find that he has to pay back the monies he has received under s 127 if a winding up order is subsequently made on his petition at the request of another creditor.

Sometimes a petitioner is asked to withdraw his petition in return for a promise by the company that it will proceed to a creditors' voluntary winding up. It must be remembered that such liquidation commences on the day the members pass the resolution to wind up whereas, if a winding up order is made on the petition of a creditor, the winding up commences on the date the petition was presented. Withdrawal of the petition could therefore lead to the loss of certain remedies for the benefit of all creditors in relation to payments made by the company after the date of presentation of the petition and before the resolution to wind up.

2 Substitution of petitioning creditor

The court may substitute as petitioner, on terms which it thinks just, any creditor or contributory who, in the court's opinion, would have a right to present a petition and who wants to prosecute the petition (r 4.19(2)). This discretion may be exercised when a petitioner for a winding up order is not entitled to present a petition (eg, because of some technical defect in his demand for payment under s 123(a)). Also where a petitioner:

(a) fails to advertise his petition within the time prescribed, or

(b) consents to withdraw his petition or to allow it to be dismissed or the hearing to be adjourned or fails to appear in support of his petition, or

(c) if appearing does not apply for an order in the terms of the prayer of his petition,

the court may substitute another creditor or contributory as petitioner (r 4.19(1)). An order to substitute a petitioner may, where a petitioner fails to advertise his petition within the time prescribed or consents to withdraw his petition, be made at any time (r 4.19(3)).

If more than one creditor seeks to be substituted, the court may direct that the creditor with the larger debt is to be substituted.

For form of precedent for summons for leave to be substituted, see the Appendix, Form 26.

A substitution order will usually direct amendment of the petition by the substitution of the new petitioner and of particulars of his debt. The amended petition should be verified by a fresh affidavit from the new petitioner and the amended petition served on the company. It is not necessary for the amended petition to be re-advertised. It will be appreciated that if the substitution takes place as a result of a hearing before the date originally fixed for the hearing of the original petition, then that hearing may proceed unaltered. However, care must be taken to ensure that the various time limits for service and advertisement set out in r 4.11 are complied with. Care should also be taken to ensure that the original petitioner had complied with the requirements of r 4.14 (see below) and if he has not, then the substituted petitioner must do so.

If substitution is ordered as a result of application made at the hearing of the petition, then the foregoing requirements will still have to be met and of necessity a new hearing date for the petition will be fixed. Again, care should be taken if the original petitioner has failed to comply with the requirements of r 4.14 to ensure that the requirements are complied with before the new hearing date. It will be necessary for the substituted petitioner to obtain certain documents from the original petitioner, such as the original petition and copies of the *London Gazette* advertisement together with affidavits of service, though in the absence of co-operation from the original petitioner, the substituted petitioner should be able to obtain the necessary documents by himself.

3 Certificate of compliance with the Rules

After a petition has been presented, the petitioner or his solicitor must, at least five days before the hearing, file at court a certificate of compliance with the Rules relating to service and advertisement (r 4.14(1)). The certificate must show the dates of presentation of the petition, of the hearing, of service and of advertisement and a copy of the advertisement must be filed (r 4.14(2)). Non compliance with this rule is a ground on which the court may dismiss the petition (r 4.14(3)). There is a form of certificate of compliance in Sched 4 to the Rules, form 4.7, see the Appendix, Form 27.

4 Notice by persons who intend to appear

Every person who intends to appear on the hearing of a petition must give the petitioner notice of his intention to do so (r 4.16(1)). The notice must contain the name and address of the person intending to appear, whether it is his intention to support or oppose the petition and the amount and nature of his debt (r 4.16(2)). There is a form of such notice in Sched 4 to the Rules, form 4.9, see the Appendix, Form 28.

Creditors frequently give notice supporting or opposing the petitioner (which does not leave them liable for any costs, as opposed to actually appearing to support or oppose). If a creditor is represented by the same solicitor as the petitioning creditor, he need not give this notice but must ensure that his name appears on the list which the petitioning creditor is required to lodge.

The notice must be sent by post so as to reach the addressee not later than 4 pm on the business day before the hearing (r 4.16(4)). A person who has failed to comply with this rule will not, without leave of the court, be allowed to appear on the hearing of the petition (r 4.16(5)).

5 List of persons who intend to appear

The petitioner or his solicitor or his London agent must prepare a list of all the names and addresses of the persons who have given notice of their intention to appear on the hearing of the petition and of their respective solicitors (r 4.17(1)). Against each name must be stated whether it is the creditor's intention to support or oppose the petition (r 4.17(2)). There is a form of such a list in Sched 4 to the Rules, see the Appendix, Form 29.

Those who have given notice of support or opposition but who do not intend to appear are also sometimes placed on this list. On the day appointed for the hearing of the petition, a fair copy of the list must be handed by the petitioner or his solicitor or London agent to the court prior to the hearing of the petition (r 4.17(3)). If no person has indicated his intention of supporting or opposing the petition, the form should have a statement to this effect written across it and signed by the petitioner, his solicitor or London agent and handed in in the same way.

The name of any person intending to appear on the hearing of the petition and employing the same solicitor as the petitioner should be included on the list.

6 Affidavits in opposition

If the company intends to oppose the petition, its affidavits must be filed not less than seven days before the hearing and a copy must be sent to the petitioner (r 4.18). There is now no time limit relating to affidavits in reply.

Chapter 6

The Hearing and the Winding Up Order

1 Powers of the court on hearing the petition

On hearing a winding up petition, the court may dismiss it, or adjourn the hearing conditionally or unconditionally, or make any interim order, or any other order that it thinks fit. However the court must not refuse to make a winding up order on the ground that the assets of the company have been mortgaged to an amount equal to or in excess of those assets or that the company has no assets (s 125(1)). Where a company is being wound up voluntarily, the court must not make a winding up order unless it is satisfied winding up cannot be continued with due regard to the interests of creditors or contributories (s 124(1)).

Where the petition is presented by members of the company as contributories on the ground that it is just and equitable that the company should be wound up, the court, if it is of the opinion:

(*a*) that the petitioners are entitled to relief either by winding up the company or by some other means; and

(*b*) that in the absence of any other remedy it would be just and equitable that the company should be wound up:

must make a winding up order. However, it does not have to make an order if it is also of the opinion both that some other remedy is available to the petitioners and that they are acting unreasonably in seeking to have the company wound up instead of pursuing that other remedy (s 125(2)).

2 Adjournment of hearing

An adjournment of the hearing at the request of the company and against the wishes of the petitioner will only be rarely granted. A creditor, unpaid at the time of the hearing, is entitled to a winding up order *ex debito justitiae* and it is no reason for an adjournment for the company to say that, given time, the creditor will be paid. It is usual to allow a short adjournment when a director seeks to appear on behalf of the company and to oppose the petition because only solicitor and counsel can appear on behalf of the company and time will be needed for the director to instruct lawyers.

An adjournment will usually be allowed when the company appears and states its intention of disputing the debt or of applying for any judgment upon which the petition is based to be set aside.

Even where the petitioner consents to the application for an adjournment by the company, the court will usually not allow more than a short adjournment of a week or so. Whilst a petition may be adjourned to enable the petitioner to consider some proposals for payment made by the company, the court will not allow a petition to be adjourned either for a lengthy period or to be adjourned on a number of occasions to enable the company to pay the petitioner's debt by instalments. The proceedings are not to be like the sword of Damocles hanging over the head of the company, waiting to drop if the company fails to meet its promise of payment by instalment.

The petitioner under such circumstances will be put to the choice of allowing his petition to be dismissed and receiving payments by instalments or of proceeding to obtain a winding up order. The petitioner is also at risk that some other creditor, having given notice of his intention to appear at the hearing of the petition, will seek leave to be substituted as the petitioning creditor, in the event of the original petitioner agreeing to the petition being dismissed, and the substituted petitioner will then proceed to seek a winding up order, after he has amended the petition and served the same on the company, at some later hearing. The original petitioner, perhaps having received all his debt by then, will be faced with having to repay what he has received to the liquidator under s 127. The repayment which would have to be made would not only be the debt itself but perhaps also the costs which the company had been persuaded to pay as a condition of the agreement with the original petitioner.

Different considerations as to the grant of adjournments would apply if such were sought, not by the company or the petitioner, but by opposing creditors. Section 195 provides that the court may have regard in all matters relating to the winding up of a company to the wishes of creditors or contributories of the company and may, if it thinks fit, even direct that meetings of the creditors or contributories should be called and that a report of the result thereof should be given to the court. The section, in effect, gives the court complete discretion in deciding what weight should be attached to the wishes of creditors and contributories. The wishes of these classes of interested parties are not to be disregarded arbitrarily but their wishes are but one of the factors which the court must bear in mind when deciding what action to take and what order to make.

3 Whether an order to wind up should be made

Assuming that the petitioner can substantiate the grounds for seeking a winding up order in accordance with his petition and there are no procedural or technical reasons why an order should not be made, then a winding up order should be made on a creditor's petition *ex debito justitiae*. But if an overwhelming majority of creditors oppose the petition, regard should be had to their wishes. Regard, under s 195, should be had to the value of each creditor's debt and the number of votes conferred on each contributory (in the case of a contributory's petition opposed by other contributories) but this is not conclusive of the outcome. Regard must also be had to the 'quality' of debts or votes on each side. For example, if one of the major creditors opposing the petition was also a director and shareholder, less weight would be attached to his opposition than to an independent outside creditor for the same amount. An example of a case where a winding up order was refused is *Re Brendacot* ((1986) 2 BCC 99/64) where the directors were conducting an informal winding up with the approval of the majority of the creditors.

There have been many cases where winding up orders have been made against the wishes of the majority of creditors. The wishes of creditors are normally expressed by their appearance at the hearing although s 195 requires their wishes to be proved to the court 'by any sufficient evidence'. Affidavits, though in some cases helpful, are not therefore essential, as they would only state the same information as that contained in the list lodged at court together with their reasons for not wanting a winding up order which will, no doubt, be expressed orally on their behalf by counsel at the hearing. The quality as well as the quantity of the opposition is also relevant. Thus, the opposition of connected parties will not be given as much weight as the views of the independent creditors eg, *Re Holiday Stamps Ltd* (1984) 82 LSG 2817; see also Chapter 2.

When a company is already in voluntary liquidation, a winding up order will not be made unless the court is satisfied that the voluntary liquidation cannot be continued with due regard to the interests of creditors and contributories (s 124(5)). It is therefore necessary for the petitioner to show some special reason or circumstance justifying the making of a winding up order. This is normally done in the affidavit in reply. A good example of a sufficient reason used to be where the voluntary liquidator had not taken all necessary steps to collect in the assets of the company and to distribute them to the various classes of creditors (eg, *Hewitt Brannan Tools* (1990) BCC 354). However, with the new provisions making it easier to remove a liquidator and all liquidators now being qualified insolvency practitioners, duly licensed and bonded, such reason may no longer be sufficient.

The voluntary liquidator may appear at the hearing and give impartial evidence on the present position of the company but not to press a view one way or the other (*Re Medisco Equipment Ltd* (1983) I BCC 98944).

4 Costs

If the petition is dimissed, the usual order will be that the petitioner must pay the company's costs. In addition, the petitioner will have to pay one set of costs to any contributories or creditors (as the case may be) who supported the winning side. The petitioner will, however, be entitled to the return of the deposit paid on issue under r 4.7(3) by virtue of art 11 of the Insolvency Fees Order 1986.

If the petition succeeds, the practice is to give costs to the petitioner and the company out of the company's estate. Similarly, one set of costs of contributories or creditors (supporting the winning side) will also be given out of the company's estate.

If a creditor knows that a winding up petition has already been presented and rather than support the first petitioner, he presents a second winding up petition, he does so at the risk of having his petition dismissed with costs. Advertisement of a winding up petition is deemed to be notice to the world and the rule about the costs of a second petition will apply to any petition presented after the date when the first petition was advertised even though the second petitioner was unaware of its existence. There is no similar procedure to that in bankruptcy for searching for prior petitions. Enquiry of the court to which it is proposed to present a petition is unlikely to be of any help since there are up to ten different courts in which a winding up petition can be legitimately presented for any company registered in England and Wales. The problem is further exacerbated by the fact that petitions are no longer advertised in local newspapers but only in the *London Gazette*, which is not read by most practitioners on a daily basis.

However, enquiries can be made of the Central Index of Winding Up Petitions at the Companies Court in London by telephoning 071 430 0630 to ascertain if there is a winding up petition pending against the company and in any court in England or Wales, there is therefore less likely to be sympathy for a second petitioner's application for costs.

The normal rules as to costs may be departed from so that a petitioner, though he failed in his petition, may be ordered to pay another party's costs and may even be awarded costs out of the company's estate himself.

Persons appearing on the petition are not entitled to share in costs unless they have given notice as required by the rules of their intention to appear or have been given special leave by the court.

If a company is already in voluntary liquidation, the voluntary liquidator is entitled to his costs if he appears on the petition to give impartial evidence on the present position of the company so as to assist the court (*Re Medisco Equipment Ltd* (1983) I BCC 98944).

A provisional liquidator is not entitled to appear on the petition save in exceptional circumstances and if he does appear, he may not get his costs.

The taxed costs of the petitioner including the taxed costs of any person appearing on the petition whose costs are allowed by the court are no longer first in priority to be paid out of the company's assets but are still high up on the list of priority (r 4.218).

Where costs are ordered to be paid out of the assets of the company, the person in whose favour such an order has been made can agree those costs with the liquidator without the necessity for those costs to be taxed (r 7.34(1)) but the court may order costs to be taxed (r 7.34(2)). The prudent thing to do would seem to be to seek an order for costs to be taxed if not agreed. If a bill for taxation is required, it will be taxed on the standard basis in accordance with the normal rules in litigation unless the court orders costs on an indemnity basis because of some special factors affecting the matter. For precedents of various forms of bills of costs, see the Appendix, Forms 44 to 46.

Once drafted, the bills of costs (if a winding up order has been made and costs have been ordered to be taxed and paid out of the assets of the company) should be sent to the Official Receiver if he is still the liquidator or if no meeting of creditors and contributories has yet taken place, or to the liquidator as the case may be. He will usually endorse the bill as approved subject to taxation and will waive notice of the date for taxation. It is then for the presenter of the bill to justify his bill before the taxing officer, though of course the Official Receiver or liquidator does have the right to appear on the bill and to object. This procedure will only, presumably, apply where the liquidator himself would have been prepared to agree costs but he has been required by the liquidation committee to require the costs to be taxed or where the court has ordered costs to be taxed without the alternative of agreement being specified.

As with all orders for costs when applied for on behalf of VAT registered clients, VAT should not be claimed. Instead, a bill for the VAT element of the costs should be sent to the petitioner by his solicitors and reclaimed by the petitioner as input tax.

5 The order

When an order for the winding up of a company has been made, the court must forthwith send to the Official Receiver a notice (form 4.13 in Sched 4 to the Rules) to this effect (r 4.20(1)). Schedule 4 also contains two forms of winding up order, form 4.11 and form 4.12 (winding up following discharge of an administration order), see the Appendix, Forms 30 and 31.

The order is prepared by the court. It is the duty of the petitioner, his solicitor or London agent and of all other persons who have appeared on the hearing of the petition to leave at the court all the documents required for the purpose of enabling the court to complete the order forthwith. This must be done at the latest on the business day after an order for the winding up of a company is pronounced in court (r 4.20(2)). It is not necessary for the court to make an appointment to settle the order unless there are any special circumstances (r 4.20(3)).

The order is drafted by the court, sent to the petitioner for his approval, and then engrossed. In some courts, the practice is to require the petitioner to engross the order. In other courts, the practice is for the court to engross the order as well. In such cases, the court sends a duplicate to the petitioner.

It is the court's duty to send three copies of the winding up order to the Official Receiver (who becomes the company's provisional liquidator automatically on the making of a winding up order) (r 4.21(1)) and it is the Official Receiver's duty to serve the order on the company, inform the Registrar of Companies and advertise the making of the order in a local newspaper and the *London Gazette* (r 4.21(2)–(4)).

For form of order dismissing the petition, see the Appendix, Form 32.

6 Rescission of the order

If the petitioner or the company wishes to apply for the winding up to be rescinded, for example, where the petitioner's debt was paid on the day of the hearing or where it is subsequently discovered that a winding up order had already been made by another court of competent jurisdiction unbeknown to the petitioner, then application must be made promptly. The applicant for rescission must inform the court which made the order and give notice to the Official Receiver and to all parties who were heard on the petition. The application must be supported by an affidavit as to the company's assets and liabilities, except in the case of an application to rescind a second winding up order because of the making of an earlier one. The application must be made within seven days of the winding up order (r 7.47(4)) but the court has power to extend time (r 4.3) though if it is made later, then the affidavit in support should also set out the reasons for the delay. In *Re Virgo Systems Ltd* (1989) 5 BCC 833, the application to rescind was made within seven days of the directors learning of the winding up order and was a case where all creditors were going to be paid in full and promptly; accordingly the winding up order was rescinded.

It should be noted that once a winding up order has been drafted, passed and entered on the court records, it cannot be rescinded.

7 Appeals

An order made on a winding up petition is, of course, subject to appeal and the practice is to treat such appeals as appeals from interlocutory order in order to secure an early hearing, although a winding up order by its very nature would appear to be a final order. Leave to appeal is therefore required (r 7.47(2)).

Any creditor or contributory, though he be the petitioner may appeal, although the Court of Appeal refuses to hear creditors and contributories in support of an appeal but will hear them in opposition to any appeal.

Where the company appeals against the making of a winding up order, it is really the directors who are making the appeal, and should the appeal be unsuccessful, the costs of the unsuccessful appellants will not normally be ordered out of the company's assets. Security for costs of the company's appeal can be ordered under the Companies Act 1985, s 726, as with all other forms of litigation pursued by a company. If the appeal is successful and the winding up order is discharged, the petitioner may be ordered to pay not only the company's costs of opposing the petition and prosecuting the appeal but also the Official Receiver's costs occasioned by the appeal including his fees and expenses as a result of his having been the provisional liquidator of the company from the date of the original winding up order until the determination of the appeal. These costs will usually be calculated on a full indemnity basis.

Chapter 7

Matters arising after Winding Up

1 Proceedings against the company

When a winding up order has been made (or a provisional liquidator appointed) no action or proceeding may be commenced or
continued against the company except with leave of the court
subject to such terms as the court may impose (s 130(2)).

2 Liquidator immediately after the order

Immediately after the making of a winding up order, the Official
Receiver becomes the provisional liquidator of the company even
if some other person had been appointed provisional liquidator
at some stage after the presentation of the winding up petition.
The Official Receiver continues to act as provisional liquidator
until he or another person becomes liquidator and is capable of
acting as such (s 136(2)).

Where a winding up order is made immediately upon the
discharge of an administration order, the court may order that
the administrator be the liquidator of the company (s 140(1)).
Similarly where a voluntary arrangement was in force at the time
of the making of the winding up order, the supervisor may be
appointed by the court as liquidator (s 140(2)). In both these
cases, the Official Receiver does not become the provisional
liquidator nor does he have the duty to summon meetings under
s 136 (s 140(3)) as set out below.

3 Official Receiver's duties

As soon as practicable in the 12 week period after the making of a winding up order, the Official Receiver must decide whether or not to summon meetings of creditors and contributories for the purpose of choosing someone to be the liquidator of the company in his place (s 136(4) and (5)), unless the court has already appointed the liquidator as set out in the foregoing paragraph. If he decides to summon such meetings, the meetings must be held not more than four months from the date of the winding up order (r 4.50(1)) and the Official Receiver must inform the court and give at least 21 days notice to all creditors and contributories (r 4.50(2) and (3)). Notice must also be given by public advertisement (r 4.50(5)). Where the Official Receiver receives a request for meetings of creditors and contributories to be held in a case where he had decided not to summon such meetings, he must withdraw any notices given by him that he did not intend to summon such meetings and fix a date and venue for the meetings not more than three months from the date of the request and proceed as if he had decided to summon meetings. Additional notices must be given in the case of banks or licensed institutions under the Banking Act 1987. The form of request for such meetings is to be found in Sched 4 to the Rules as form 4.21.

If the Official Receiver decides not to summon meetings, he must inform the court, creditors and contributories and tell them of their right to requisition meetings provided 25 per cent in value of them want him to (s 136(5)(*b*) and *c*)). The Secretary of State can appoint a person to be liquidator at any time when the Official Receiver is liquidator (s 137) and thus, as the Official Receiver becomes liquidator (not provisional liquidator) automatically on the making of a winding up order, the Secretary of State can make an appointment once the winding up order is made. His choice is not the subject of approval or otherwise of creditors if a meeting of creditors is subsequently summoned.

It is the Official Receiver's duty to investigate the causes of the company's failure and generally the promotion, formation, business dealings and affairs of the company and to make such report (if any) to the court as he thinks fit (s 132(1)).

The Official Receiver may require the officers or former officers of the company to submit a sworn statement of affairs in the prescribed form (form 4.17 in Sched 4 to the Rules). If the Official Receiver gives a notice requiring a statement of affairs to be submitted, it must be submitted within 21 days or such longer period as the Official Receiver may allow (s 134(4) and (5)).

4 Notice of the first meeting of creditors and contributories

Notice of the first meeting of creditors and contributories must be given to all creditors and contributories individually unless the court orders that notice need only be given by advertisement having regard to cost, the value of assets of the company and the interests of creditors (r 4.59). The forms of notice are set out in Sched 4 to the Rules as forms 4.22 (creditors) and 4.23 (contributories), see the Appendix, Forms 33 and 34.

In fixing the venue of a meeting, the Official Receiver must have regard to the convenience of those who are to attend (r 4.60(1)) and meetings must be held between 10 am and 4 pm on business days unless the court orders otherwise (r 4.60(2)). With every notice summoning a meeting there must be included forms of proxy (form 8.4 in Sched 4 to the Rules, see the Appendix, Form 35).

The notice to creditors must state a time and date not more than four days before the meeting by which the creditors must lodge their proofs of debt and, if applicable, proxies in order to entitle them to vote at the first meeting (r 4.50(4)). The Official Receiver must give at least 21 days' notice of these meetings to any personnel of the company whom he wishes to attend these meetings (r 4.58(2)).

5 Rules governing meetings

(1) The Official Receiver (or someone nominated in writing by him) is the chairman of the first meetings. Once a liquidator is appointed, he chairs meetings.

(2) At a meeting of creditors, a resolution is deemed to be passed when a majority in value of the creditors present personally or by proxy have voted in favour of the resolution. At a

meeting of contributories, a resolution is deemed to be passed when a majority in value of the contributories present personally and by proxy have voted in favour of the resolution, the value of the contributories being determined by the number of votes conferred upon each contributory by the articles of association (r 4.63(1)).

(3) It is necessary for there to be a quorum of creditors and contributories for their respective meetings to be effective. In the case of a creditors' meeting, the quorum is one creditor in person or by proxy. In the case of a contributories' meeting, the quorum is two. But if the chairman is aware from proxies or proofs lodged that some more people are coming to the meeting, he must wait for 15 minutes after the due time before starting the meeting (r 12.4A). If there is no quorum, then the only business that can be transacted is the election of a chairman, the proving of debts and the adjournment of the meeting. If there is no quorum present within half an hour of the time appointed for the meeting, it must be adjourned for not more than 21 days (r 4.65(5)) to such a date and place as the chairman thinks fit (r 4.65(4)).

(4) No creditor can vote at any meeting unless he has lodged with the Official Receiver not later than the time mentioned for this purpose in the notice convening the meeting a proof of debt, that is, a statement in the appropriate form (see Chapter 8) of the amount claimed by him as due to him and the claim has been admitted for the purpose of entitlement to vote (r 4.67(1)(a)). Acceptance by the Official Receiver of a proof of debt for voting purposes is not the same as acceptance of a proof by the ultimate liquidator to rank for dividend. Creditors are not allowed to vote if their debts are unliquidated or contingent nor if their debts are secured (r 4.67(3) and (4)). For the purposes of voting, a secured creditor may value his security and vote for the excess of his debt over the security held. If the chairman agrees to put an estimated minimum value on an unascertained debt, the claimant of such a debt can vote for that value (r 4.67(3)).

(5) The Official Receiver as chairman of the meeting can decide to reject a proof for voting purposes but that decision is subject to appeal (r 4.70). If the Official Receiver is in doubt as to the validity of a claim, he should mark the proof and allow the creditor to vote subject to his vote being subsequently declared invalid if the objection is sustained (r 4.70(3)). If on

appeal, the Official Receiver's decision to reject a proof is reversed, the court may order a further meeting (r 4.70(4)).

(6) Where the chairman holds a proxy requiring him to vote for a particular resolution, if no one else proposes that resolution, he must do so unless he considers that there is good reason for not doing so (r 4.64).

6 Proxies

(a) Need for a proxy

A creditor or a contributory may vote either in person or by proxy. Only a sole trader or other individual creditor can appear in person. If such a creditor wishes to appoint another person to attend a meeting on his behalf, he too must give the person attending his proxy. All other entities, that is, partnerships, companies or corporations, can only vote via a representative authorised to vote on their behalf by a proxy form (r 4.67(1)(b)). The court may in exceptional circumstances allow otherwise (r 4.67(2)).

Where a person is authorised by the Companies Act 1985, s 375 to represent a corporation or company at any meeting of creditors or contributories, he must produce to the Official Receiver a copy of the resolution so authorising him. That copy must either be under the seal of the corporation or company or must be certified to be a true copy by the secretary or a director of that organisation (r 8.7).

It is the practice for companies to authorise a representative to attend and vote on their behalf or to vote in a particular way by completing a proxy form signed by the secretary or director and sealed by the company or signed by some person indicating that he is duly authorised under the seal of the company to sign the proxy form on behalf of the company. Strictly speaking this practice does not accord with r 8.7 and is therefore incorrect. Though there is no appeal procedure laid down if the chairman of the meeting rejects a proxy duly lodged and therefore does not allow that creditor's vote, it is open to the creditor affected to apply to the court for the chairman's decision to be reversed and for a new meeting to be held by analogy to the principle laid down in the case of *Re Palmer Marine Survey Ltd* (1985) *The Times*, 26 October.

(b) Form of proxy

Proxy forms must be sent out to creditors and contributories with the notice summoning their meetings (r 8.2(1)) and no form of proxy can be used except the one sent out with the notice or a substantially similar one (r 8.2(2)). Schedule 4 to the Rules includes forms of proxy for use in connection with meetings following a winding up order, form 8.3, see the Appendix, Form 35.

Neither the name nor the description of the Official Receiver or liquidator or any other person may be printed or inserted in the body of any proxy form before it is sent out (r 8.2(1)).

A creditor or contributory may give a proxy to any person of full age (who himself need not be a creditor or contributory) (r 8.1(3)) requiring the proxy holder to use his discretion on voting (a general proxy) or requiring him to vote for or against any specified resolution (a special proxy). A creditor or contributory may appoint the Official Receiver to be his general or special proxy. If the Official Receiver or other chairman has a number of general proxies given to him, it is usual for him to vote with these proxies in accordance with the wishes of the majority as expressed at the meetings themselves or by virtue of special proxies lodged.

(c) Lodging proxies

A proxy which the holder intends to use at any meeting of creditors or contributories must be lodged with the Official Receiver not later than the time mentioned for that purpose in the notice convening the meeting or the adjourned meeting. That time must be not more than four business days before the date fixed for the meeting (r 4.54(4)). Faxed proxies will not be accepted by the Official Receiver.

(d) Solicitation for proxies and voting by proxy holders

Where the court is satisfied that any improper solicitation has been used by or on behalf of a liquidator in obtaining proxies or in procuring his appointment as liquidator, it may order that no remuneration be allowed to the person by whom or on whose behalf the solicitation was exercised (r 4.150(1)). This is so notwithstanding any resolution of the liquidation committee or of the creditors to the contrary (r 4.150(2)).

No person acting under a proxy may vote in favour of any resolution which would directly or indirectly place him or any associate of his in a position to receive any remuneration out of the estate of the company (r 8.6(1)). However, where any person holds proxies requiring him to vote for the appointment of himself as liquidator he may use those proxies and vote accordingly (r 8.6(1)).

It is a criminal offence to offer or to give to a creditor or contributory any financial inducement to vote for or against the appointment of a particular person as liquidator (s 164).

7 Business at the first meetings

The primary purpose of such meetings is to appoint a liquidator. In fact, pursuant to r 4.52, no resolutions can be taken at the meeting of creditors other than:

  (*a*) a resolution to appoint a named insolvency practitioner to be liquidator or two or more insolvency practitioners as joint liquidators;
  (*b*) a resolution to establish a liquidation committee;
  (*c*) (unless a liquidation committee has been established) a resolution specifying the terms of the liquidator's remuneration or to defer consideration of that matter;
  (*d*) if two or more liquidators are appointed, a resolution specifying whether acts are to be done by both or all of them or by only one;
  (*e*) a resolution adjourning the meeting for not more than three weeks; and
  (*f*) any other resolutions which the chairman thinks it right to allow for special reasons.

The same applies to the contributories' meeting except no resolution regarding the liquidator's remuneration can be passed. At neither meeting can any resolution be proposed which has as its object the appointment of the Official Receiver as liquidator (r 4.52(3)). Thus, the Official Receiver will only become the liquidator of the company if no nominations for the appointment of a liquidator are put forward and the Official Receiver does not decide to ask the Secretary of State (under s 137) to appoint another person as liquidator.

The Official Receiver as convener of such meetings can require the company's personnel to attend these meetings (r 4.58) and so it must be presumed that matters regarding the company's activities can be raised by either the Official Receiver or those present.

If the meetings of creditors and contributories do not vote for the appointment of the same person as liquidator, then any creditor or contributory can apply to the court within seven days of the meetings for the court to make any appointment it thinks fit (s 139(4)).

If there is a number of nominations for the position of liquidator, then a vote is taken in accordance with the rules as set out in section 5(4) above but if there are three or more nominees, the chairman must continue taking votes until one nominee has a clear majority with the nominee obtaining the least support dropping out each time (r 4.63(2)).

No person can be appointed as liquidator unless he is a qualified insolvency practitioner. Qualified insolvency practitioners are those who hold licences from the various authorised professional bodies (such as those governing Chartered Accountants and Certified Accountants, the Law Society or the Insolvency Practitioners Association) or from the Department of Trade.

The liquidation committee of creditors and contributories is appointed (except where the Official Receiver is liquidator) to assist the liquidator generally and in particular to determine the liquidator's remuneration, though this power is subject to the overriding jurisdiction of creditors generally and the court (see Chapter 9 for further details of the duties and functions of the liquidation committee).

8 Certifying the appointment of liquidator

The Official Receiver or whoever is the chairman of the meetings must certify the appointment of the liquidator but not until the person appointed has provided him with a written statement that he is a qualified insolvency practitioner and consents to act (r 4.100(2)). The Official Receiver must file the certificate at court and the liquidator's appointment is effective from the date on which it is certified (r 4.100(4)). The Official Receiver must send a copy of the certificate endorsed with the date of filing to the liquidator (r 4.100(5)).

There is no longer any requirement for the liquidator to provide a separate fidelity bond for each appointment as liquidator which he holds.

9 Resignation of liquidator and vacancies

A liquidator may resign his office (in the prescribed circumstances) by giving notice to the court (s 172(6)). Before resigning, the liquidator must call a meeting of creditors (and non contributories as well) and the notice of the meeting must be accompanied by an account of his administration (r 4.108). A liquidator may only resign because of ill-health, ceasing to be a qualified insolvency practitioner or because of some conflict of interest (r 4.108(4)). Where two or more liquidators were originally appointed, any one can seek to resign if he and the others are of the opinion that it is no longer expedient to have that number of joint liquidators (r 4.108(5)).

Notice of the meeting must also be given to the Official Receiver and the chairman of the meeting must inform the Official Receiver of the resolutions passed at the meeting, viz, to accept the resignation of the liquidator, that a new liquidator be appointed and that the resigning liquidator be or be not given his release (r 4.109(2)). The liquidator's resignation is effective from the date the notice of it is filed by the Official Receiver at court (r 4.109(6)). If the creditors refuse to accept the liquidator's resignation, the court may, on the liquidator's application, give him leave to resign (r 4.111).

During any vacancy in the post of liquidator (such as that caused by the death of the liquidator), the Official Receiver is by virtue of his office the liquidator (s 136(3)). He must then decide whether or not to summon meetings of creditors and contributories to replace the liquidator having regard to the stage in the administration reached by the previous liquidator (s 136(4)). If one quarter in value of the creditors request him to convene a meeting to appoint a new liquidator, he must do so (s 136(5)(c)).

10 Removal of liquidator

A liquidator can be removed by resolution of the creditors at a meeting duly summoned of which proper notice specifying the purpose of the meeting has been given. Someone other than the liquidator or his nominee may be elected chairman but if the liquidator is the chairman, he may not adjourn the meeting without the consent of at least half in value of those present (in person or by proxy) and entitled to vote (r 4.113(3)). If the liquidator is removed, the creditors can also resolve not to give him his release.

If the liquidator does not summon a meeting to consider the resolution to remove him, the court can order such a meeting to be held and give directions as to the way it is to be conducted (r 4.119). However, if an application is made to the court for an order requiring the liquidator to summon a meeting to consider a resolution for his removal as liquidator, the court may, if it thinks no sufficient cause has been shown for the application, dismiss it but not until after an *ex parte* hearing of the applicant (r 4.119(2)). If the court considers the application should proceed, a date will be fixed.

The court can remove a liquidator on the application of an interested person and r 4.119(2) applies to such an application as well.

The Secretary of State can remove a liquidator but before doing so must notify the liquidator and the Official Receiver of his decision and his reasons and specify a period within which the liquidator can make representations against his removal (r 4.123).

In all the above cases, the liquidator removed from office may or may not be given his release.

Chapter 8

Proofs of Debt and Dividends

1 Mode and form of proof

In a winding up by the court, every person claiming to be a creditor must prove his claim in writing to the liquidator (r 4.73) unless the court orders otherwise (r 4.67(2)). This is called proving a debt and the document by which the creditor seeks to establish his claim is his proof (r 4.73(3)). A proof must be in the form known as 'proof of debt' whether the form prescribed by the Rules and set out in Sched 4 to the Rules as form 4.25 or a substantially similar form—see the Appendix, Form 36 and must be signed by the creditor or someone authorised on his behalf (r 4.73(4)). Government departments do not have to use this form provided they give all the information required.

Proof of debt forms must be sent out by the Official Receiver or liquidator to every creditor who is known to him or identified in the statement of affairs (r 4.74). If the Official Receiver decides not to summon a meeting of creditors, he must nonetheless send out proofs of debt with the notice of his decision. If he decides to call a meeting, then the proofs of debt must be sent with the notice convening the meeting. If the liquidator is appointed by the court, he must send out proofs of debt with notice of his appointment (r 4.74(2)).

The liquidator may require a proof of debt to be verified by affidavit in the form set out in Sched 4 to the Rules or a substantially similar form (form 4.26—see the Appendix, Form 37). Such an affidavit can be sworn by the creditor before his own solicitor (r 7.57).

2 Provable debts

All claims by creditors are provable as debts against the company whether they are present or future, certain or contingent, ascertained or sounding only in damages (r 12.3). Formerly unliquidated damages in tort were not provable debts but they are now covered by the wide nature of r 12.3.

However, any sum due to a contributory by way of dividend, profits or otherwise is not deemed to be a debt of the company *pari passu* with other debts but can rank as a deferred debt (s 74(2)(*f*)). Dividends which have not been paid to a parent company cannot be regarded as having been paid and lent back so as to create a debt (*Re L B Holliday Ltd* [1986] 2 All ER 367).

3 Contents of proof

The following must be stated in a proof of debt (r 4.75(1)):
- (*a*) the creditor's name and address:
- (*b*) the total amount of the debt as at the date the company went into liquidation – note, not the date of the commencement of liquidation, that is, the date of presentation of the petition (s 129(2)) but the date of the winding up order or resolution to wind up voluntarily if earlier (s 247(2));
- (*c*) is interest included;
- (*d*) is VAT included;
- (*e*) is any part of the debt a preferential debt as defined in s 386 and Sched 6 to the Act;
- (*f*) particulars of how and when the debt was incurred;
- (*g*) particulars of any security held and if so, its value;
- (*h*) the name, address and authority of person signing, if not the creditor himself;
- (*i*) any documents which can substantiate the claim though these need not be sent unless the liquidator requests them (r 4.75(2)); and
- (*j*) if the debt was incurred in a foreign currency, the sterling equivalent at the date the company went into liquidation (see the note to (*b*) above) must be calculated and stated

(r 4.91) and the rate of exchange used must be the official rate, ie, that fixed by the Bank of England or by the court.

4 Debt payable at a future date and of a periodic nature

If a creditor is owed a debt not payable at the date the company went into liquidation, he may nonetheless prove for the same (r 4.94) but subject to an adjustment of his dividend where payment of the dividend is made before the time when the debt would have become payable. See r 11.13 for the method of calculation of the adjustment.

In the case of rent and other payments of a periodic nature, the creditor may prove for any amounts due and unpaid up to the date the company went into liquidation (r 4.92(1)). Where at that date any payment accruing was due where payment in arrears was stipulated, the creditor may prove for the amount which would have fallen due if the debt had accrued from day to day (r 4.92(2)).

5 Bills of exchange and promissory notes

Unless the liquidator allows otherwise, a proof in respect of money owed on a bill of exchange, promissory note or other negotiable instrument or security upon which the company is liable cannot be admitted for any purpose, unless the document or a certified copy is produced (r 4.87).

6 Time for proofs

There is no time limit for the submission of proofs of debt though the court may fix a time within which creditors are to prove their debts or be excluded from the benefit of any distribution made before those debts are proved (s 153). Also until such time as a creditor has lodged a proof of debt, he cannot vote at meetings of creditors.

Before declaring a dividend, the liquidator must give notice of his intention to do so to all creditors of whom he is aware or who are identified in the statement of affairs who have not proved their debts (r 11.2(1)). The notice must specify the last date for proving which must be not less than 21 days after the date of the notice (r 11.2(2)). The notice must also state the liquidator's intention to declare a dividend (specified as interim or final) within the period of four months from the last date for proving (r 11.2(3)). The notice must be advertised unless the liquidator has previously advertised for creditors to prove their debts (r 11.2(1A)).

Only those creditors who have proved their debts can receive any dividend.

7 Admission and rejection of proofs

The liquidator must examine every proof of debt and admit it wholly or in part for dividend. If he rejects a proof in whole or in part, he must give his reasons in writing and inform the creditor concerned (r 4.82). The liquidator must within seven days of the last date for proving (see above) deal with every creditor's proof by admitting it or rejecting it in whole or in part or by making such provision as he thinks fit in respect of it (r 11.3(1)). He is not obliged to deal with proofs lodged after the last date for proving but may do so if he thinks fit (r 11.3(2)). The liquidator must estimate the value of any debt subject to any contingency or which for any other reason does not bear a certain value and he may revise any estimate made because of change of circumstances or further information becoming available to him (r 4.86). He must inform the creditor of his estimate.

Acceptance of a proof of debt for voting purposes at the first meeting is not the same as acceptance by the liquidator of a proof for dividend and the liquidator is not bound by the earlier decision of the Official Receiver.

If a creditor is dissatisfied with the decision of the liquidator, the court may on the application of the creditor reverse or vary the liquidator's decision (r 4.83). However, subject to the power of the court to extend the time under r 4.3, no application to reverse or vary the decision of the liquidator in a winding up by the court rejecting a proof will be entertained unless notice of the application is given before the expiration of 21 days from the date of service of the notice of rejection (r 4.83). If the creditor makes application for time to be extended, the liquidator would be entitled to be heard. For form of notice of rejection, see the Appendix, Form 38. For forms of summons or notice of motion, affidavit in support and order, see the Appendix, Forms 39 to 41.

8 Expunging proofs

The court may expunge or vary a proof which has been admitted either upon the application of the liquidator (or of a creditor or contributory, if the liquidator declines to interfere) (r 4.85).

9 Interest

(a) Up to the date company went into liquidation

Where a debt proved in a liquidation bears interest (be it contractual or statutory) interest up to the date the company went into liquidation can also be proved for (r 4.93(1)). Even if the proved debt did not include the right to interest, interest can be claimed up to the date the company went into liquidation if:

(i) by virtue of a written instrument and in respect of a debt payable at a certain time, then from that time (r 4.93(3)) at judgment rate applicable at the date of liquidation (r 4.93(6));

(ii) otherwise, after demand for repayment has been made stating that interest will thereafter be charged (r 4.93(4)) at the rate specified in the notice provided that it does not exceed judgment rate applicable at the date of liquidation (r 4.93(6)).

Any interest due on debts which are preferential under s 386 and Sched 6 to the Act would not appear also to be preferential.

(b) After the date the company went into liquidation

If there is a surplus remaining after paying all proved debts (including interest on them up to the date the company went into liquidation), it must be applied to the payment of interest on all proved debts (including any interest thereon up to the date the company went into liquidation) before any other purpose (s 189(2)). All debts for the purpose of entitlement to interest under this section rank equally, ie, preferential debts do not have preferential rights to interest. The rate of interest allowable is the greater of contractual and judgment rate of interest.

10 VAT

A creditor whose claim includes an element of VAT can either prove for the whole amount of the claim (and pay to HM Customs and Excise the VAT element irrespective of whether or not he receives any dividend) or prove for the amount of his claim net of VAT and reclaim the VAT under the VAT Bad Debt Relief Regulations 1978 as amended. When a liquidator sent out a notice calling for proofs of debt, he usually also sent out a VAT Bad Debt Relief Form pursuant to these regulations, on which he would certify that a claim has been submitted to him and this allows the creditor to reclaim the VAT element. For a precedent of such form, see the Appendix, Form 43. However, as a result of changes introduced in 1990 and by the Finance Act 1991, VAT Bad Debt Relief is now only obtainable in respect of goods or services supplied after 26 July 1990 at the expiration of 12 months from the tax point, provided the debt has been written off in the creditor's books. Liquidation (or any other insolvency proceedings) are now no longer relevant to the claiming of VAT Bad Debt Relief. In the event that the liquidator is able to pay 100p in the pound to creditors and still has funds available, creditors are not under any duty then to seek to claim, in addition, the VAT so as to pay it over to HM Customs and Excise (*Re T H Knitwear Ltd* (1986) *The Times*, 8 November).

11 Secured creditors

A secured creditor may, with the agreement of the liquidator or leave of the court, at any time alter the value which he has, in his proof of debt, placed upon his security but if he is the petitioner for the winding up of the company or has voted in respect of his unsecured balance, he may revalue his security only with the leave of the court (r 4.95).

If a secured creditor omits to disclose his security in his proof of debt, he must surrender it for the general benefit of creditors unless the court relieves him on the ground that omission was inadvertent or the result of honest mistake (r 4.96).

The liquidator may at any time give notice to a secured creditor that he proposes at the end of 28 days to redeem the security at the value placed upon it by the creditor in his proof. The creditor then has 21 days in which, if he so wishes, to revalue his security (subject to r 4.95). The secured creditor has the right to call upon the liquidator to elect whether or not to exercise his power to redeem and the liquidator then has six months in which to exercise the power or decide not to exercise it (r 4.97(4)).

If the liquidator is dissatisfied with the value placed on the security, he can call upon the creditor to offer the security for sale (r 4.98). When the security is ultimately realised, the net proceeds must be substituted for any value previously put upon it (r 4.99).

12 Dividends

The liquidator must give notice of a dividend to all creditors who have proved their debts (r 11.6(1)). The notice, which can be sent out with the dividend itself, must include the following particulars:

(*a*) amounts realised from the sale of assets;
(*b*) payments made by the liquidator in the administration of the liquidation;
(*c*) provision for unsettled claims and funds retained for particular purposes;
(*d*) the total amount to be distributed and the rate of dividend; and
(*e*) whether, and if so when, any further dividend is expected to be declared (r 11.6(2)).

Dividends may be sent by post, held for collection or paid in some other way (r 11.6(4)). A creditor can assign his right to a dividend and give notice to the liquidator of this whereupon the liquidator must pay the dividend to the assignee (r 11.11). For a precedent of such an authority, see the Appendix, Form 42.

The liquidator must not, except with the leave of the court, proceed to declare a dividend whilst there is pending any application to the court to reverse or vary a decision of his on a proof or to expunge a proof or to reduce the amount claimed (r 11.5(2)). If the court gives leave, the liquidator must make provision in respect of the proof in question as the court directs.

If the liquidator is unable to declare any or any further dividend, he must give notice to this effect to creditors and the notice must also contain a statement to the effect that no funds have been realised or that all funds realised have been distributed or used to meet the expenses of the liquidation (r 11.7).

A creditor who failed to lodge his proof before an interim dividend was declared is not entitled to disturb that interim distribution but is entitled to receive a payment in priority to other creditors from further funds as available; similarly a creditor whose proof is increased after an interim dividend has been declared.

A partially secured creditor is entitled to receive a dividend on the unsecured part of his claim having valued his security. If revaluation of his security is necessary, resulting in a greater shortfall, he is to be treated as the creditors referred to in the previous paragraph.

The liquidator cannot be sued for a dividend but if he refused to pay a dividend, the court may order him to pay it out of his own funds, together with, interest at judgment rate and costs (r 4.182(3)).

The liquidator when declaring a dividend must give notice stating how the dividend is proposed to be distributed and containing such particulars as will enable the creditors to comprehend the calculations of the dividend and the manner of its distribution (r 4.180(3)).

On a final distribution, the liquidator can ignore any creditors who have not lodged proofs of debt, after receiving notice of the liquidator's intention to declare a final dividend on a specified date (r 4.186).

Chapter 9

The Liquidation Committee

1 Membership and establishment of the committee

Any creditor (other than a secured creditor) is eligible to be a member of the committee provided that he has lodged a proof of debt and his proof has not been wholly disallowed for voting purposes nor for the purposes of distribution and dividend (r 4.152(3)).

A body corporate may be a member of the committee (r 4.152(5)) but it can only act through a representative duly authorised in accordance with r 4.159. This requires the representative to hold a letter of authority from the member, entitling him so to act and signed by or on behalf of the committee member (r 4.159(2)).

The liquidation committee must consist of at least three and not more than five creditors (together with up to three contributories if the company is being wound up other than because of inability to pay its debts) (r 4.152) but contributory members' rights as members of the committee are secondary to creditor members and their votes do not count in the same way unless and until all creditors have been paid in full.

The liquidation committee does not come into being until the liquidator has issued a certificate of its due constitution (r 4.153) and his certificate must not be issued until he has received the written consent to act from the minimum number of members of the committee (r 4.153(3A)).

If a creditors committee was established under s 26 to assist the administrator after the making of an administration order, and a winding up order was made immediately upon the discharge of the administration order, the creditors committee becomes the liquidation committee provided that the minimum number of three members have been maintained, none of whom are secured and the liquidator issues a certificate of due constitution (r 4.174–6).

2 Functions and rights of the committee

The main function of the liquidation committee is to determine the remuneration of the liquidator (r 4.127(3)). It can determine that the liquidator should be paid a percentage of the value of the assets realised and/or distributed or by reference to the time spent by the liquidator and his staff and must have regard, in arriving at its determination, to the complexity or otherwise of the matter, any exceptional responsibility falling on the liquidator, the liquidator's effectiveness and the value and nature of the assets dealt with by the liquidator. If the committee resolves that a liquidator who has used improper solicitation to obtain proxies or to procure his appointment as liquidator, should nonetheless receive remuneration for acting as liquidator, the court can override this resolution (r 4.150).

Schedule 4 to the Act sets out a number of powers which a liquidator can only exercise with sanction. Where there is a committee, it is that committee from whom sanction must be sought in the first instance. These powers are:

(*a*) to pay any class of creditors in full;

(*b*) to compromise calls and claims between the company and any contributories;

(*c*) to make any compromise with creditors or persons claiming to be creditors;

(*d*) to bring or defend proceedings in the name of the company;

(*e*) to carry on the business of the company so far as may be necessary for the beneficial winding up of the company.

It is the duty of the committee to review the adequacy of the liquidator's security (r 12.8).

It is the duty of the liquidator to report to the committee all such matters as appear to him or as the committee have indicated to him to be of concern to them with respect to the winding up (r 4.155(1)). The liquidator need not comply with any request for information where it appears to him that the request is frivolous or unreasonable or the cost of complying would be excessive or there are not sufficient assets to meet the cost of complying (r 4.155(2)). The liquidator must send a report to every member of the committee setting out the position generally regarding the progress of his administration. Such reports must be sent not less than once every six months or as and when directed by the committee but not more often than once every two months (r 4.168).

3 Meetings of the committee

The first meeting of the committee must take place within three months of its establishment and thereafter within 21 days of a request for a meeting by a member of the committee or on the date previously resolved by the committee for a further meeting (r 4.156(2)). Meetings are to be held otherwise when and where determined by the liquidator (r 4.156(1)).

The liquidator is to chair meetings of the committee but he may nominate someone else to stand in for him and that person must either be an employee of his experienced in insolvency matters or another qualified insolvency practitioner (r 4.157).

The quorum for meetings of the committee is two (r 4.158). A member of the committee can be represented by someone else provided that person is holding a letter of authority duly signed by the member (r 4.159).

4 Resolutions by post

The liquidator can seek to obtain the agreement of members of the committee to a resolution by sending to every member a copy of the proposed resolution (r 4.167(1)). Each resolution must be set out in such a way that agreement can be indicated to each resolution. Any members of the committee can within seven business days of the resolution being sent out require the liquidator to summon a meeting to consider the matters raised by the resolution (r 4.167(3)). In the absence of such a request, the resolution is deemed to have been passed if and when the liquidator is notified in writing by a majority of the members that they concur (r 4.167(5)).

5 Termination of membership and vacancies

A committee member may resign by notice in writing to the liquidator (r 4.160).

A person's membership of the committee is automatically terminated:

(*a*) if he becomes bankrupt (his trustee replaces him) or he compounds with his creditors;

(*b*) if he is not present or represented at three consecutive meetings (unless at the third meeting it is resolved that this rule will not apply); and

(*c*) if he ceases to be or is found never to have been a creditor (r 4.161).

A committee member may be removed by resolution of the creditors (or contributories as the case may be) at a meeting of which 14 days' notice has been given.

If a vacancy on the committee exists, then:

(*a*) it need not be filled if the liquidator and a majority of the remaining members so agree;

(*b*) the liquidator may appoint some other creditor to be a member if the majority of the remaining members so agree; or

(*c*) a meeting of creditors should be convened so that another creditor can be appointed and 14 days' notice of such meeting must be given (r 4.163).

6 Dealings with committee members

No member of the committee, his representative or associate of them, nor any person who was a member of the committee in the last 12 months may enter into any transaction whereby he receives out of the company's assets any payment for services given or goods supplied in connection with the administration, or obtains any profit from the administrations, or acquires any asset forming part of the estate (r 4.170(2)) except with leave of the court, with prior sanction of the committee where full value for the transaction is given and in cases of urgency, or by way of performance of a contract in existence at the date of liquidation, where leave of the court is sought subsequently without delay (r 4.170(3)).

No member of the committee, his representative or associate may vote on any resolution to sanction any such transactions (r 4.170(4)).

7 Expenses of members

Members of the committee are entitled to receive any travelling expenses directly incurred by them or their representatives in attending committee meetings or otherwise acting on the committee's business (r 4.169). These expenses are payable out of the assets of the company in the order of priority prescribed in r 4.218, subject to the jurisdiction of the court under s 156 to make an order as to the payment of the expenses incurred in the winding up in such order of priority as it thinks fit.

8 No committee

Where there is no committee and the liquidator is other than the Official Receiver, the functions of such a committee are vested in the Secretary of State except to the extent that the Rules otherwise provide (s 141(5)).

Chapter 10

Rights of Creditors

Once a winding up order has been made, creditors have the right to choose the liquidator if the Official Receiver decides to summon a meeting of creditors for this purpose. If the Official Receiver decides not to summon such a meeting, creditors have the right to request that the Official Receiver does summon such a meeting provided that the request is properly made by at least one quarter in value of the creditors (r 4.50).

At the meeting of creditors, creditors can elect a liquidation committee but if no liquidation committee is established, it is creditors who have the right to fix the liquidator's remuneration. For more relating to these matters, see Chapter 7.

The right of creditors to remove a liquidator whom they believe is not doing his job well is now more clearly set out in the Act and the Rules. If the liquidator agrees at the request of at least one quarter in value of all non associated creditors to summon a meeting to consider his removal, a simple majority of those creditors present and voting will be sufficient to oust the liquidator. Creditors can also decide whether or not the ousted liquidator should be given his release. If the liquidator declines to summon such a meeting, then an application to the court can be made, but good reason for the application will have to be shown if the court is to make an order, see Chapter 7 section 10.

Creditors have the right to lodge their claims (prove their debts) for voting and dividend purposes and if they feel that their proofs of debt have not been fairly treated, there is an appeal procedure laid down (see Chapter 8, section 7). If creditors feel that the liquidator has wrongly admitted a claim for dividend, they can apply to the court for that creditor's proof of debt to be expunged (see Chapter 8, section 8).

Interest on debts can be claimed up to the date of liquidation and even after it if the assets of the company are sufficient to pay all creditors' proved debts in full (see Chapter 8, section 9).

It is no longer possible for creditors to apply to the court for directors or other officers of the company to be examined by the court as to the company's dealings. Only the liquidator has the power under s 236 (private examination of officers). However, under s 133 if one half in value of the company's creditors request the liquidator to apply to the court for the public examination of company officers (directors, administrators, liquidators or others) then he must do so.

Only the liquidator can bring proceedings alleging voidable preference, fraudulent trading or wrongful trading. However, under s 212 the court may, on the application of the liquidator or any creditor, examine the conduct of any officer and compel him to restore to the company any money or property misapplied. Creditors can apply to the court for an order requiring the liquidator to make a report to the Director of Public Prosecutions with the object that consideration be given to the prosecution of past or present officers of the company for any criminal offence in relation to his actions relating to the company (s 218).

The 'victim' of any transaction entered into by the company at an undervalue is one of the persons who can make application to the court for that transaction to be set aside (s 423). This would seem to include any of the company's creditors.

The liquidator is under an obligation under s 192 to make returns to the Registrar of Companies and creditors can, of course, inspect these returns at the Companies Registry. The liquidator is required to provide a list of creditors to any creditor requesting the same, on payment of a fee, unless the statement of affairs has been filed, in which case creditors can obtain a copy from the court (r 12.17).

With each dividend received, creditors must also be given sufficient information to enable them to comprehend how their dividend was calculated (r 4.80(3)).

The liquidator is under a duty to convene a meeting of creditors if requisitioned by at least one quarter in value of the creditors.

The Official Receiver is under a duty to send out to all creditors a report containing a summary of the statement of affairs amplified, modified or explained as he thinks fit (r 4.45). This duty must be observed irrespective of whether the Official Receiver decides to summon a meeting of creditors to appoint a liquidator.

Appendix

Forms

(Numbers in brackets refer to the form number in Sched 4 to the Rules)

1 Statutory demand under s 123(1)(*a*) or 221(1)(*a*) of the Insolvency Act 1986 (4.1)

2 General title

3 Winding up petition (general form) (4.2)

4 Winding up petition (resolution by company)

5 Winding up petition (by unpaid creditor on simple debt)

6 Winding up petition (by unpaid creditor after statutory demand)

7 Winding up petition (by judgment creditor levying execution)

8 Winding up petition (by creditor on inability to pay debts)

9 Winding up petition (just and equitable/deadlock)

10 Winding up petition (when voluntary winding up already in existence)

11 Winding up petition (by contributory) (4.14)

12 Affidavit verifying winding up petition (4.3)

13 Affidavit of service of winding up petition at registered office (4.4)

14 Affidavit of service of winding up petition other than at registered office, or on an oversea company (4.5)

15 Advertisement of winding up petition (4.6)

16 Notice of motion for order restraining advertisement of and proceeding with petition

17 Order granting interim injunction restraining advertisement of petition (on *ex parte* application)

18 Order granting injunction restraining advertisement of petition and directing removal of petition from file

19 Summons for appointment of provisional liquidator

20 Affidavit supporting summons for appointment of provisional liquidator

21 Order of appointment of provisional liquidator (4.15)

22 Examples of additional powers sometimes given to provisional liquidator

23 Consent to act as provisional liquidator or liquidator

24 Order of appointment of special manager (4.60)

25 Order for leave to withdraw winding up petition (4.8)

26 Summons for leave to be substituted as petitioner

27 Certificate that relevant provisions of Rules have been complied with (4.7)

28 Notice of intention to appear on petition (4.9)

29 List of persons intending to appear on the hearing of the petition (4.10)

30 Order for winding up by the court (4.11)

31 Order for winding up by the court following upon the discharge of an administration order (4.12)

32 Order dismissing petition with costs against the petitioner

33 Notice to creditors of meeting of creditors (4.22)

34 Notice to contributories of meeting of contributories (4.23)

35 Proxy (winding up by the court) (8.4)

36 Proof of debt (general form) (4.25)

37 Affidavit of debt (4.26)

38 Rejection of proof

39 Summons or notice of motion to reverse or vary liquidator's decision on proof

40 Affidavit in support of summons to reverse liquidator's decision on proof

41 Order reversing or varying rejection of proof or giving leave to amend proof

42 Authority to liquidator to pay dividends to another person

43 VAT Bad Debt Relief form

44 Petition's bill of costs of a petition to wind up

45 Company's bill of costs of petition to wind up

46 Creditor's or contributory's bill of costs of petition to wind up

Form 1 Statutory demand under section 123(1)(a) or 222(1)(a) of the Insolvency Act 1986
(*see p 8 Prescribed Form 4.1*)

Warning
- This is an **important** document. This demand must be dealt with **within 21 days** after its service upon the company or a winding-up order could be made in respect of the company.
- Please read the demand and notes carefully.

Notes for Creditor
- If the creditor is entitled to the debt by way of assignment, details of the original creditor and any intermediary assignees should be given in part B on page 3.
- If the amount of debt includes interest not previously notified to the company as included in its liability, details should be given, including the grounds upon which interest is charged. The amount of interest must be shown separately.
- Any other charge accruing due from time to time may be claimed. The amount or rate of the charge must be identified and the grounds on which it is claimed must be stated.
- In either case the amount claimed must be limited to that which has accrued due at the date of the demand.
- If signatory of the demand is a solicitor or other agent of the creditor the name of his/her firm should be given.

Demand

To _____

Address _____

_____

This demand is served on you by the creditor:

Name _____

Address _____

_____

The creditor claims that the company owes the sum of £_____ , full particulars of which are set out on page 2.

The creditor demands that the company do pay the above debt or secure or compound for it to the creditor's satisfaction.

Signature of individual _____

Name _____
(BLOCK LETTERS)

Date _____

*Position with or relationship to creditor _____

_____

*Delete if signed by the creditor himself

*I am authorised to make this demand on the creditor's behalf.

Address _____

_____

Tel. No. _____   Ref. _____

N.B. The person making this demand must complete the whole of this page, page 2 and parts A and B (as applicable) on page 3.

FORMS

Particulars of Debt.
(These particulars must include (a) when the debt was incurred, (b) the consideration for the debt (or if there is no consideration the way in which it arose) and (c) the amount due as at the date of this demand.)

Notes for Creditor
Please make sure that you have read the notes on page 1 before completing this page.

Note:
If space is insufficient continue on reverse of page 3 and clearly indicate on this page that you are doing so.

PART A

The individual or individuals to whom any communication regarding this demand may be addressed is/are:—

Name _____   _____
(BLOCK LETTERS)
Address _____   _____

_____   _____

Telephone Number _____   _____

Reference _____   _____

PART B

For completion if the creditor is entitled to the debt by way of assignment

	Name	Date(s) of Assignment
Original creditor		
Assignees		

How to comply with a statutory demand

If the company wishes to avoid a winding-up petition being presented it must pay the debt shown on page 1, particulars of which are set out on page 2 of this notice, within the period of **21 days after** its service upon the company. Alternatively, the company can attempt to come to a settlement with the creditor. To do this the company should:

- inform the individual (or one of the individuals) named in part A above immediately that it is willing and able to offer security for the debt to the creditor's satisfaction; or
- inform the individual (or one of the individuals) named in part A immediately that it is willing and able to compound for the debt to the creditor's satisfaction.

If the company disputes the demand in whole or in part it should:

- contact the individual (or one of the individuals) named in part A immediately.

REMEMBER! The company has only 21 days after the date of service on it of this document before the creditor may present a winding-up petition.

Form 2 General Title

(*Royal Arms—on petitions and other originating process only*)
In the High Court of Justice
Chancery Division
Companies Court [*or*   District Registry]
[*or* In the Ambridge County Court]

                              No   of 19

In the Matter of XYZ Limited
               and
In the Matter of the Insolvency Act 1986

Form 3 Winding-up petition (general petition)
(*see p 14 Prescribed Form 4.2*)

(TITLE)

(a) Insert title of court   To (a)

(b) Insert full name(s) and address(es) of petitioner(s)   The petition of (b)

(c) Insert full name of company subject to petition   1. (c)

(hereinafter called "the company") was incorporated on

(d) Insert date of incorporation   (d)

under the Companies Act 19

(e) Insert address of registered office   2. The registered office of the company is at (e)

3. The nominal capital of the company is £
divided into   shares of £   each. The amount of the capital paid up or credited as paid up is £

4. The principal objects for which the company was established are as follows:

and other objects stated in the memorandum of association of the company

(f) Set out the grounds on which a winding-up order is sought   5. (f)

6. In the circumstances it is just and equitable that the company should be wound up
The petitioner(s) therefore pray(s) as follows:—

(1) that (c)

may be wound up by the court under the provisions of the Insolvency Act 1986
or

(2) that such other order may be made as the court thinks fit.

FORMS

(g) If the company is the petitioner, delete "the company". Add the full name and address of any other person on whom it is intended to serve this petition

Note: It is intended to serve this petition on (g) [the company] [and]

Endorsement

(h) Delete as applicable

(j) Insert name and address of Court
(k) Insert name and address of District Registry

This petition having been presented to the court
on _____will be heard at (h) [Royal Courts of Justice, Strand, London WC2A 2LL] [(j) _____ County Court
_____]
[(k) _____ District Registry _____]
on:

Date _____

Time _____ hours _____
(or as soon thereafter as the petition can be heard)

The solicitor to the petitioner is:—

Name _____

Address _____
_____

Telephone no. _____

Reference _____

(h) [Whose London Agents are:—

Name _____

Address _____
_____

Telephone no. _____

Reference _____]

Form 4   Winding up petition (resolution by company)
(see p 14)

(Title as in Form 2)

Paragraphs 1, 2, 3 and 4 as in Form 3.
5. At an Extraordinary General Meeting of the company duly convened and held on   the following resolution was duly passed as a Special Resolution in accordance with section 378 of the Companies Act 1985 namely:

> 'That the company be wound up by the court and that the directors of the company be authorised to present a petition to the court on behalf and in the name of the company and to take all other necessary steps for that purpose.'

The petitioner therefore *(continue as in Form 3)*

Form 5   Winding up petition (by unpaid creditor on simple debt)
(see p 14)

(Title as in Form 2)

Paragraphs 1, 2, 3 and 4 as in Form 3.

5. The company is indebted to the petitioner in the sum of £   for *(state the consideration for the debt with particulars so as to establish that the debt claimed is due)*

6. The petitioner has made application to the company for payment of his debt, but the company has failed to pay the same or any part thereof.

7. The company is [insolvent and] unable to pay its debts.

8. In the circumstances, it is just and equitable that the company should be wound up.

The petitioner therefore *(continue as in Form 3)*

Form 6   Winding up petition (by unpaid creditor after statutory demand)
(see p 14)

(Title as in Form 2)

Paragraphs 1, 2, 3 and 4 as in Form 3.
5. *(as in Form 5)*
6. On   19   the petitioner served on the company by leaving it at the registered office of the company aforesaid a statutory demand requiring the company to pay the said sum which demand was in the following terms:

(Here set out Form 1)

7. Over three weeks have now elapsed since the petitioner served the said demand but the company has neglected to pay or satisfy the said sum or any part thereof or to make any offer to the petitioner to secure or compound the same.
8. The company is [insolvent and] unable to pay its debts.
9. In the circumstances, it is just and equitable that the company should be wound up.
The petitioner therefore *(continue as in Form 3)*

Form 7 Winding up petition (by judgment creditor levying execution)
         (*see p 14*)

(*Title as in Form 2*)

Paragraphs 1, 2, 3 and 4 as in Form 3.

5. The company is indebted to the petitioner in the sum of £
being as to £   the amount of a final judgment obtained by the
petitioner against the company in the   Court on   19
and as to £   the costs of obtaining the said judgment. The
consideration for the said judgment was the price of goods sold
and delivered by the petitioner to the company on   19   [*or
as the case may be*]

6. On   19   the petitioner issued a writ of fieri facias upon
the said judgment and the said execution was duly made by the
sheriff of   on   19 .

7. The petitioner has received notice from the said sheriff that the
company has indicated its inability to pay out the execution and
intended therefore to proceed to an auction of the company's
assets but that he has received information that all or nearly all of
the company's assets are held by the company on lease and in
addition, the sheriff holds other writs of execution totalling £   .
In the circumstances the petitioner decided to withdraw.

Or

7. On   19   the sheriff of   returned the same wholly
unsatisfied as the company had no goods or chattels within his
bailiwick [*or* County] upon which execution could be levied.

Or

6. On   19   the petitioner issued a warrant of execution
upon the said judgment.

7. On   19   the Registrar of the   County Court made
a return to the said execution that the same had been levied on
the goods of the company and the sale of such goods had realised
the sum of £   and the sum of £   being the balance of the
amount of the said judgment remained unsatisfied.

Then

8. The said judgment remains [wholly unpaid and unsatisfied and
the amount] [*or* unpaid and unsatisfied to the extent of £   and
such sum] is still justly due and owing to the petitioner.

9. The company is [insolvent and] unable to pay its debts.

10. In the circumstances it is just and equitable that the company
should be wound up.

The petitioner therefore (*continue as in Form 3*)

Form 8   Winding up petition (by creditor on inability to pay debts)

(see p 14)

(Title as in Form 2)

Paragraphs 1, 2, 3 and 4 as in Form 3.

5. *(as in Form 5)*.

6. *(as in Form 5)*.

7. On or about   19   the company created a debenture in favour of   Bank Plc to secure the principal sum amounting to £   charging the whole of the company's undertaking and all property whatsoever and wheresoever present and future, including uncalled capital for the time being.

8. On   19   in pursuance of the terms contained in the said debenture,   was appointed Receiver and Manager of the assets and undertaking of the company by the said   Bank Plc.

Or

7. In reply to a letter by the petitioner requesting payment of the said debt, the petitioner received a letter from the company [*or* its solicitors *or* its accountants] (*or as the case may be*) stating that the company had not assets with which to meet the said debt.

Or

7. The petitioner attended a meeting with directors of the company on   19   at which the said directors stated that the company had no or not sufficient assets with which to meet the said debt.

Then

[8 *or* 9]. The said sum of £   is still justly due and owing to your petitioner.

[9 *or* 10]. The company is [insolvent and] unable to pay its debts.

[10 *or* 11]. In the circumstances, it is just and equitable that the company should be wound up.

The petitioner therefore (*continue as in Form 3*)

Form 9   Winding up petition (just and equitable/deadlock)
(*see p 14*)

(*Title as in Form 2*)

Paragraphs 1, 2, 3 and 4 as in Form 2.

5. (*Here set out the division of share capital between the petitioner and other members and how the business of the company has been conducted if no single member of the company had voting control.*)

6. The petitioner and   are the sole directors of the company.

7. Until recently the company has been trading very successfully and if there was a winding up, there would be a surplus for members.

8. In   19   difference arose between the petitioner and the only other director as to how the business should be run. The petitioner did not wish certain contracts to be entered into but   as the only director wished these contracts to be undertaken by the company. Since this disagreement, it has not been possible to agree on any matters relating to the operation of the business of the company including the payment to the directors of remuneration for their services.

9. On   19   a Board Meeting was held but   left the meeting before important and urgent business could be transacted. It has therefore become impossible to conduct the business of the company for under the Articles of Association of the company the petitioner has no power to act alone on behalf of the board of directors.

10. In the circumstances, it is just and equitable that the company should be wound up.

The petitioner therefore (*continue as in Form 3*)

Form 10   Winding up petition (when voluntary winding up already in existence)
(see p 14)

(Title as in Form 2)

Paragraphs 1, 2 3 and 4 as in Form 3.
5. The company is indebted to the petitioner for the sum of £
for goods sold and delivered by the petitioner to the company on
              19   but despite repeated demands the company has failed
to pay the said sum or any part thereof [*or as the case may be*]
6. On   19   at an Extraordinary General Meeting of the company a Special Resolution for the Voluntary Winding Up of the
company and for the appointment of AB as liquidator was passed.
[The said resolution was confirmed by a meeting of creditors duly
convened under the provisions of section 98 of the Insolvency Act
1986 and held on the same day.]
7. The assets of the company including the premises of the company were sold by the said AB as such liquidatition on or about
              19   for the sum of £
8. The company is insolvent and unable to pay its debts but there
should be a substantial dividend for its creditors.
9. Notwithstanding the long time since the appointment of AB as
liquidator and the realisation of the assets of the company on
              19   and repeated applications by the petitioner, the said
AB has taken no further steps in the liquidation of the company
and has given no indication that he intends to take any such steps
[*or as the case may be.*]
10. In the circumstances the voluntary winding up cannot be continued with due regard to the interests of the creditors and it is
just and equitable that the company should be wound up by the
court. The petitioner therefore (*continue as in Form 3*)
NOTE: It is intended to serve this petition on X Limited and on AB
of (*address*) the liquidator appointed in the voluntary winding up
thereof. (*conclude as in Form 3*)

Form 11 **Petition by contributory**
(*see p 14 Prescribed Form 4.14*)

(TITLE)

(a) Insert title of court To (a)

(b) Insert full name(s) and address(es) of petitioner(s) The petition of (b)

(c) Insert full name of company subject to petition 1. (c)

(hereinafter called "the company") was incorporated on (d)

(d) Insert date of incorporation under the Companies Act 19

(e) Insert address of registered office 2. The registered office of the company is at (e)

3. The nominal capital of the company is £   divided into shares of £   each. The amount of the capital paid up or credited as paid up is £

(f) Delete as applicable The petitioner(s) is/are the holder(s) of shares of £   each. Such shares (f) [were allotted to him/them on the incorporation of the company] [have been registered in his/their name(s) for more than 6 months in the last 18 months] [devolved upon him/them through the death of the former holder of the shares].

4. The principal objects for which the company was established are as follows:—

and other objects stated in the memorandum of association of the company.

(g) Set out the grounds on which the petition is presented 5. (g)

6. In the circumstances it is just and equitable that the company should be wound up.

The petitioner(s) therefore pray(s) as follows:—

(1) that (c)

may be wound up by the court under the provisions of the Insolvency Act 1986

OR

(2) that such other order may be made as the court thinks fit.

Note:
It is intended to serve this petition on:—

ENDORSEMENT

This petition having been presented to the court on _____
let all parties attend before the Registrar in Chambers on

Date _____

Time _____ hours

Place _____
for directions to be given.

The solicitor(s) for the petitioner is/are:

Name _____

Address _____

_____

Telephone No. _____

Reference _____

(h) [Whose London agents are:—

Name _____

Address _____

_____

Telephone No. _____

Reference _____]

(h) Delete if London agents not instructed

Form 12   Affidavit verifying winding up petition
(*see p 17   Prescribed Form 4.3*)

(TITLE)

(a) Insert name and address of person making oath

I (a)

Make oath and say as follows:—

(b) Delete if affidavit not made by Petitioner in person

1. (b)   I am the Petitioner. The statements in the Petition now produced and shown to me marked "A" are (c) [true] [true to the best of my knowledge, information and belief].

(c) Delete as applicable

1. (d)   I am (e)
of the Petitioner.

(d) Delete if affidavit is made by Petitioner in person

2. (d)   I am duly authorised by the Petitioner to make this affidavit on (c) [its] [his] behalf.

(e) State capacity eg. director, secretary, solicitor etc

3. (d)   I have been concerned in the matters giving rise to the Petition and have the requisite knowledge of the matters referred to in the Petition because (f)

(f) State means of knowledge of matters sworn to in affidavit

4. (d)   The statements in the Petition now produced and shown to me marked "A" are (c) [true] [true to the best of my knowledge, information and belief].

Sworn at

Form 13 Affidavit of service of winding up petition at registered office

(see p 16 Prescribed Form 4.4)

Note: If the petition was served on an officer or an employee of the company use Part A of this form. If it was served on a person authorised to accept service on behalf of the company use Part B. If it was served by depositing it at the registered office use Part C.

(TITLE)

I (a)

make oath and say as follows:—

(a) Insert name, address and description of person making oath

(b) Insert date

(c) Delete as applicable

Part A.
That I did on (b)
serve the above-named company with a sealed copy of the petition now produced and shown to me marked "A" by handing the same to _____ (c) [who acknowledged himself to be] [who is to the best of my knowledge, information and belief] (c) [a director] [an officer] [an employee] of the company at (d)

the registered office of the said company.

OR
Part B.
That I did on (b)
serve the above-named company with a sealed copy of the petition now produced and shown to me marked "A" by handing the same to _____ who acknowledged to me that he was authorised to accept service of documents on behalf of the company at (d)

(d) Insert address of registered office

the registered office of the said company.

OR
Part C.
That I did on (b)
having failed to find any officer, employee or other person authorised to accept service of documents on behalf of the company, deposit a sealed copy of the petition now produced and shown to me marked "A" at (d)

(e) Insert where the petition was left in such a way that it was likely to come to the attention of a person attending the registered office e.g. on a desk, through the letter box, affixed to the above, etc.

the registered office of the said company by leaving it (e)

Sworn at

Form 14 Affidavit of service of winding up petition other than at registered office or on an oversea company
(*see p 16 Prescribed Form 4.5*)

Note: If the petition was served on an officer or on an employee of the company use Part A of this form. If it was served on a person authorised to accept service on behalf of the company use Part B.
If the petition was served on an oversea company use Part C only

(a) Insert name, address and description of person making oath

(b) State reason why petition has been served at an address other than a registered office

(c) Insert date

(d) Delete as applicable

(e) Insert address at which service effected

(f) Insert class of postage

(g) Insert name

(TITLE)

I (a)

make oath and say as follows

1. (b)

Part A

2. That I did on (c)   serve the above named company with a sealed copy of the petition now produced and shown to me marked "A" by handing the same to   (d) [who acknowledged himself to be] [who is to the best of my knowledge, information and belief] (d) [a director] [an officer] [an employee] of the company at (e)

(d) [the company's last known principal place of business in England and Wales] [a place where the company carried on business in England and Wales]

or
Part B

2. That I did on (c)   serve, the above-named company with a sealed copy of the petition now produced and shown to me marked "A" by handing the same to   who acknowledged to me that he was authorised to accept service of documents on behalf of the company at (e)

(d) [the company's last known principal place of business in England and Wales] [a place where the company carried on business in England and Wales].

or
Part C

That I did on (c)   serve the above named company with a sealed copy of the petition now produced and shown to me marked "A" by (d) [leaving it] [sending it by (f)   post] to (e)

(d) [the address of (g)
whose name has been delivered to the Registrar of Companies as a person authorised to accept on the said company's behalf service of process and any notices required to be served on it] [a place of business established by the said company in Great Britain].

Sworn at

Form 15 Advertisement of winding up petition
(*see p 17 Prescribed Form 4.6*)

(TITLE)

(a) Insert registered office address of company, or (if an unregistered company) the address of its principal place of business, or (if an oversea company) the address at which service of the petition was effected.

A Petition to wind up the above-named company of (a)

presented on (b)

(b) Insert date   by (c)

(c) Insert name and address of petitioner.

(d) Delete where the petition is presented by the company itself, or by a person who is not a creditor or contributory.

(d) [Claiming to be a (e) [creditor] [contributory] of the company] will be heard at (e) [The Royal Courts of Justice, Strand, London WC2A 2LL] [_____ County Court at _____] [_____ District Registry at _____]

(e) Delete as applicable   Date _____

Time _____ hours
(or as soon thereafter as the petition can be heard)

(f) Insert date, which should be the business day before that appointed for the hearing

Any person intending to appear on the hearing of the petition (whether to support or oppose it) must give notice of intention to do so to the petitioner or his/its solicitor in accordance with Rule 4.16 by 16.00 hours on (f)

The petitioner's solicitor is (g)

(g) Where applicable insert name and address of solicitor

Dated _____

Form 16 Notice of motion for order restraining advertisement of and proceeding with petition
(*see p 21*)

(*Title as in Form 2*)

TAKE NOTICE that this Court will be moved before [the Honourable Mr Justice   ] sitting at [the Royal Courts of Justice, Strand, London WC2A 2LL (*or as the case may be*)] on   day the   day of   199 at   o'clock in the   noon or so soon thereafter as Counsel can be heard, by Counsel on behalf of the above mentioned   Limited whose registered office is situate at (*address*) for an Order:

(1) that A.B. the Petitioner named in the Petition herein which was preferred unto this Honourable Court on   199 be restrained from taking any further proceedings upon the Petition whether by advertising the same or otherwise;

(2) that the Petition be removed from the file of proceedings; and

(3) that the Petitioner do pay the costs of this motion.

[AND TAKE NOTICE that special leave to give this short notice of motion for the day, hour and place aforesaid has been given by (the Honourable Mr Justice   )]

DATED the   day of   199

(*name and address*)

Solicitors for the above named

To (*name of Petitioner*)   and to C.D. and Co of (*address*) his solicitors.

[Adapted by kind permission of Butterworth & Co (Publishers) Ltd from Atkin's Court Forms Vol 10 (1981 Issue), title Companies—Winding Up Form 44]

Form 17   Order granting interim injunction restraining advertisement of petition (on ex parte application)
(see p 21)

(Title as in Form 2)

UPON MOTION this day made unto this Court by Counsel on behalf of the abovenamed   Limited whose registered office is situate at (*address*)

AND UPON READING the Petition preferred unto this Court in the above matters at the instance of A.B. on   199   and the Affidavit of A.B. filed   199   (*etc as the case may be*)

AND The Applicant by its Counsel undertaking to abide by any Order which this Court may make as to damages in case this Court shall be of the opinion that the said A.B. shall have sustained any by reason of this Order which the Applicant ought to pay

THIS COURT DOTH ORDER that the said A.B. be restrained until   day   199   from doing (whether by himself or his servants or agents or any of them or otherwise howsoever) the following act that is to say advertising the said Petition

AND the Applicant is to be at liberty to serve Notice of Motion for an injunction for   day   199

[Adapted by kind permission of Butterworth & Co (Publishers) Ltd from Atkin's Court Forms Vol 10 (1981 Issue), title Companies—Winding Up Form 45]

Form 18 Order granting injunction restraining advertisement of petition and directing removal of petition from file (*see p 21*)

(Title as in Form 2)

UPON MOTION this day made unto this Court by Counsel on behalf of the above named   Limited whose registered office is situate at (*address*)

AND UPON HEARING Counsel for A.B. the Petitioner named in the Petition preferred unto this Court in the above matters on

199 (the Respondent)

AND UPON READING the said Petition the Order dated 199 the Affidavit of A.B. filed   199 (*etc as the case may be*)

THIS COURT DOTH ORDER that the Respondent the said A.B. be restrained from taking (whether by himself or his servants or agents or any of them or otherwise howsoever) any further proceeding upon the said Petition whether by advertising the same or otherwise

AND IT IS ORDERED that the Petition be removed from the file of proceedings

AND IT IS ORDERED that the Respondent the said A.B. do pay the Applicant the said   Limited its costs of the Motion made unto this Court in the above matters on   199 and of this Motion such costs to be taxed.

[Adapted by kind permission of Butterworth & Co (Publishers) Ltd from Atkin's Court Forms Vol 10 (1981 Issue), title Companies—Winding Up Form 46]

Form 19 Summons for appointment of provisional liquidator
(see p 25)

(Title as in Form 2)

LET (the above named   Limited *or, if the application is ex parte*, ALL PARTIES concerned) attend at the Chambers of Mr Registrar   , Companies Court, Royal Courts of Justice, Strand, London WC2A 2LL [*or* the chambers of District Judge (*address*)] [*or* the offices of the   County Court (*address*)] on   day, the   day   199 at   o'clock in the   noon on the hearing of an application by A.B. of (*address*), the Petitioner herein, for an Order that the Official Receiver (or some other fit and proper person) be appointed as Provisional Liquidator of the above-named Company.

DATED the   day of   199

This summons was taken out by C.D. and Co of (*address*), Solicitors for the Applicant.

To (*insert name and address of persons to be served and their solicitors*)

Form 20   Affidavit supporting summons for appointment of provisional liquidator
(*see p 25*)

(*Title as in Form 2*)

1,   of   , make oath and say as follows:

1. I am the petitioner herein and crave leave to refer to the petition herein.

2. I make this affidavit in support of my application that a provisional liquidator be appointed to   Limited (hereinafter referred to as 'the company').

3. The company is insolvent with liabilities of £   and assets of only £   . The company has been in financial difficulties for some time and winding up petitions have been presented against the company before but have been withdrawn after arrangements were made with the creditors concerned.

4. I fear that if no provisional liquidator is appointed, there is a severe risk that the remaining assets of the company may be dissipated or used to pay some creditors' claims in preference to others under circumstances where the recovery of those sums wrongly paid would prove impossible. For some time Mr   , a director of the company has been in the habit of paying creditors' claims by means of endorsing over cheques received and payable to the company. Goods have also been returned to suppliers in lieu of payment of their accounts and due to lack of proper stock records of the company it would be impossible for any liquidator ultimately appointed to unravel such transactions and enable all creditors to have been treated alike. It is within my knowledge that XYZ Limited, a supplier of   to the company has received the return of stock in the recent past.

5. In the circumstances, it is necessary that a provisional liquidator should be appointed to protect the company's assets pending the hearing of the petition, with leave to borrow money so as to enable him to continue trading and any money borrowed shall be a first charge on the undertaking.

6. I have been in contact with P.L., a qualified insolvency practitioner and he has agreed to act as provisional liquidator of the company.

Sworn

Form 21 Order of appointment of provisional liquidator

(*see p 25 Prescribed Form 4.15*)

(TITLE)

(a) Give full name and address of applicants

Mr Registrar   in Chambers
Upon the application of (a)

And upon hearing

And upon reading the petition to wind up the above named company and the evidence

(b) If a person other than the official receiver is to be appointed delete the words in [ ] otherwise insert the amount to be deposited

It is ordered that (b) [upon the sum of £_____ being deposited by the applicant with the official receiver] the following person is appointed provisional liquidator of the above-named company.

Name of provisional liquidator (c) _____

(c) Insert either "the official receiver" or if an insolvency practitioner is to be appointed, his full name and address

Address (if applicable) _____

_____

_____

And it is ordered that:—

(d) Insert details of the functions to be carried out by the provisional liquidator in relation to the company's affairs

(d)

Dated _____

NOTICE TO OFFICERS OF COMPANY

You are required by Section 235 of the Insolvency Act 1986 to give the provisional liquidator all the information as he may reasonably require relating to the company's property and affairs and to attend upon him at such times as he may reasonably require.

Date _____

Form 22   Examples of additional powers sometimes given to a provisional liquidator
(*see p 25*)

AND IT IS ORDERED that the said P.L. be at liberty for the purpose of carrying on the business of the said company to borrow money AND IT IS ORDERED that the said P.L. be at liberty to execute a proper instrument or instruments whereby the amount so to be borrowed do constitute a first charge upon all the assets of the said company subject only to any existing charge thereon.
AND IT IS ORDERED THAT the said P.L. be at liberty to:
(1) Take all such steps and actions, including the pursuit of legal proceedings, as are considered by him necessary for the purpose of identifying, locating and recovering all assets, including debts and other things in action, to which the company is or appears to be entitled or has or appears to have an interest.
(2) To negotiate for and enter into a provisional contract (such contract to be subject to the approval of the court) for the sale of the business of the said company as a going concern.
(3) To negotiate for and enter into a provisional contract (such contract to be subject to the approval of the court) for the sale of the assets and undertakings of the company.

Form 23   Consent to act as provisional liquidator or liquidator
(*see p 24*)

(*Title as in Form 2*)

I, P.L. of (*address*), appointed as Provisional Liquidator of the above-named Company by Order of this Court dated   199 hereby undertake to act as such Provisional Liquidator *or* nominated as Liquidator of the abovenamed Company at the statutory meetings of Creditors and Contributories held on   199 hereby undertake to act as such Liquidator if appointed by the Court.

DATED this   day of 199

To the Official Receiver in Companies Liquidation, (*address*)

Form 24 Order of appointment of special manager
(see p 25 Prescribed Form 4.60)

(TITLE)

Mr Registrar   in chambers

(a) Insert full name and
address of applicant

Upon the application of (a) _____

_____

_____

_____

And upon hearing

And upon reading the evidence

(b) Insert full name and
address of person to
be appointed as
special manager

It is ordered that (b) _____

_____

_____

_____

(c) Give details of the
company's name and
the following:—

(i) the special
manager's
responsibility over the
company's business
or property;
(ii) the powers
entrusted to the
special manager under
section 177(4) of the
Insolvency Act 1986;

(iii) the duration of the
special manager's
appointment; and

(iv) the special
manager's
remuneration

be appointed special manager of (c) _____

_____

_____

Dated _____

Form 25 Order for leave to withdraw winding up petition
(see p 28 Prescribed Form 4.8)

(TITLE)

(a) Insert date Winding-up petition presented on (a) _____

(b) Insert name and Upon the ex parte application of (b) _____
address of applicant

_____

And upon reading _____

And upon hearing _____ ,
And the court being satisfied that the petition has not been advertised, that no notices in support of or in opposition to the petition have been received by the petitioner and that the company consents to this order
It is ordered that the petitioner be at liberty to withdraw the said petition

(c) Insert any further [and that (c) _____]
terms of the order

Dated _____

Form 26 Summons for leave to be substituted as petitioner
(see p 30)

(Title as in Form 2)

Let A.B. of (*address*), the petitioner named in the petition preferred
unto this Honourable Court in the above matter on   199
attend at the Chambers of the Registrar, Companies Court, Royal
Courts of Justice, Strand, London WC2A 2LL [*or* District Judge
        sitting in chambers at   ] on   day, the   day of
        199   on the hearing of an application by C.D. a creditor [*or*
contributory] of the abovenamed company for an order that the
applicant may be substituted as petitioner in the said petition in
place of the Respondent.
DATED (*conclude as in Form 19*)

[Adapted by kind permission of Butterworth & Co (Publishers) Ltd
from Atkin's Court Forms Vol 10 (1981 Issue), title Companies—
Winding Up Form 50]

Form 27   Certificate that relevant provisions of Rules have been complied with
(see p 31   Prescribed Form 4.7)

(TITLE)

(a) Insert date   Winding-up petition on (a)

I certify that the above-mentioned petition

which will be heard on (a)   was served in accordance with the provisions of Rule 4.8 on (a)

and advertised in accordance with the provisions of Rule 4.11 on (a)

Signed _____

Dated _____

Name in BLOCK LETTERS _____

Note A copy of the advertisement must be filed in court with this certificate.

Form 28 Notice of intention to appear on petition
(*see p 31 Prescribed Form 4.9*)

(TITLE)

(a) Insert date Winding-up petition presented on (a) _____

to be heard on (a) _____

(b) Insert full name and address, or if a firm, the name of the firm and address Take notice that (b) _____

_____

_____

(c) Delete as applicable (c) [a creditor of the above-named company for £ _____] [a contributory of the above-named company holding _____ shares in the company] intends to appear on the hearing of the above-mentioned petition to (c) [support] [oppose] it.

Signed _____

Dated _____

Position with or relationship to (c) [creditor] [contributory]

(d) If creditor or contributory's solicitor or other agent please give name and address of firm and insert name(s) and address(es) of petitioner(s) or petitioner(s) solicitor (d) _____

_____

_____

_____

To (d) _____

_____

_____

_____

Telephone No _____

Reference No _____

Form 29 List of persons intending to appear on the hearing of the petition

(*see p 31   Prescribed Form 4.10*)

(TITLE)

Winding-up petition presented on

The following persons have given notice that they intend to appear on the hearing of the above-mentioned petition on

Name and Address	Name and Address of Solicitors if any	Amount owed to creditor £	Number of shares held by contributory	Whether supporting or opposing the petition

Form 30 **Order for winding up by the court**
(*see p 39   Prescribed Form 4.11*)

(TITLE)

(a) Insert name and address of petitioner (as appropriate) "the company" or "... a creditor of the company" or "... a contributory of the company"

Upon the petition of (a)

presented to this court on

And upon hearing

And upon reading the evidence

(b) Insert full name of the company

It is ordered that (b)

be wound up by this court under the provisions of the Insolvency Act 1986

(c) Insert names of all parties to be awarded their costs

(d) Insert any terms concerning costs

And it is ordered that the costs of (c) _____

of the said petition be paid out of the assets of the company (d)

Dated _____

*Delete as appropriate

Note: [The] [One of the]* official receiver(s)* attached to the court is by virtue of this order liquidator of the company.

Form 31 Order for winding up by the court following upon the discharge of an administration order
(see p 39 Prescribed Form 4.12)

(TITLE)

(a) Delete words in brackets as applicable

(b) Insert name and address

(c) Insert date

Upon the petition of the company (a) [by its administrator (b) _____ _____] or [(b) _____ _____ a [creditor] [member] of the above-named company] [pursuant to leave of this court by order dated (c) _____] [by agreement with the administrator dated (c) _____]

presented to this court on (c)

And upon hearing

And upon reading the administration order dated (c)

and the evidence

It is ordered that the said administration order be and the same is discharged.

(d) Insert full name of company

And it is ordered that the said (d)

be wound up by this court under the provisions of the Insolvency Act 1986.

(a) [And it is ordered that _____
be appointed liquidator of the company]

(e) Insert any further items of order, eg as to costs

And it is ordered (e)

Dated _____

Form 32   Order dismissing petition with costs against the petitioner
(*see p 39*)

(*Title as in Form 2*)

UPON THE PETITION (*continue as in Form 30*)
AND UPON HEARING Counsel for the Petitioner for the said company and A.B. and   other creditors whose names are set out in the Schedule hereto respectively creditors of the said company opposing the said petition
AND UPON READING (*continue as in Form 30*)
[AND UPON HEARING the evidence of the said   and on their cross-examination and re-examination on their respective affidavits taken orally before this court on the hearing of the said petition]
THIS COURT DOTH ORDER that the said petition do stand dismissed out of this court
AND IT IS ORDERED that the Petitioner, the said   , do pay to the said   Limited and to the said A.B. and (*number*) other creditors opposing named in the said Schedule their costs of the said petition such costs to be taxed if not agreed [but on such taxation only one set of costs is to be allowed between the said   Limited and the said creditors opposing].

THE SCHEDULE BEFORE REFERRED TO

Creditors opposing the said petition

(*set out their names*)

[Adapted by kind permission of Butterworth & Co (Publishers) Ltd from Atkin's Court Forms Vol 10 (1981 Issue), title Companies— Winding Up Form 63]

Form 33   Notice to creditors of meeting of creditors
(see p 44   Prescribed Form 4.22)

(TITLE)

(a) Delete as applicable
(b) Insert relevant section

A meeting of creditors of the above-named company has been summoned by the (a) [official receiver] [liquidator] (a) [at the request of a creditor, under section (b) [   ] of the Insolvency Act 1986] for the purpose of:

The meeting will be held as follows:—

Date _____

Time _____ hours

Place _____

(c) Insert date and time by which proxy is to be lodged which should be not more than 4 days before the date fixed for the meeting

A proxy form is enclosed which must be lodged with me not later than (c) to entitle you to vote by proxy at the meeting (a) [together with a completed proof of debt form if you have not already lodged one].

Dated _____

Official Receiver/Liquidator
[address]

NOTE: Insert any further details which by the nature of the meeting need to be stated.

Form 34 Notice to contributories of meeting of contributories
(see p 44 Prescribed Form 4.23)

(TITLE)

A meeting of the contributories of the above named company

(a) Delete as applicable   has been summoned by the (a) [official receiver] [liquidator]

(b) Insert relevant   (a) [at the request of a contributory under section (b) [   ] of the
Section   Insolvency Act 1986] for the purpose of:

The meeting will be held as follows:—

Date _____

Time _____ hours

Place _____

(c) Insert date and   A proxy form is enclosed which must be lodged with me not later than
time by which proxy is   (c)
to be lodged which
should be not more   to entitle you to vote at the meeting.
than 4 days before the
date fixed for the
meeting

Dated _____

Official Receiver/Liquidator
[address]

NOTE: Insert any further details which by the nature of the meeting need to be
stated.

Form 35 Proxy (winding up by the court or bankruptcy)
(*see p 47 Prescribed Form 8.4*)

(TITLE)

Notes to help completion of the form	
Please give full name and address for communication	Name of creditor/contributory _____ Address _____ _____ _____
Please insert name of person (who must be 18 or over) or the "Official Receiver". If you wish to provide for alternative proxy-holders in the circumstances that your first choice is unable to attend please state the name(s) of the alternatives as well.	Name of proxy-holder _____ 1 _____ _____ _____ 2 _____ _____ _____ 3 _____ _____ _____
Please delete words in brackets if the proxy-holder is only to vote as directed ie he has no discretion	I appoint the above person to be my/the creditor's/contributory's proxy-holder at the meeting of creditors/contributories to be held on _____, or at any adjournment of that meeting. The proxy-holder is to propose or vote as instructed below [and in respect of any resolution for which no specific instruction is given, may vote or abstain at his/her discretion].

FORMS

111

Please complete paragraph 1 if you wish to nominate or vote for a specific person as trustee/liquidator

Voting instructions for resolutions

1. For the appointment of _____ of _____

_____

Please delete words in brackets if the proxy-holder is only to vote as directed ie he has no discretion

as liquidator of the company/trustee of the bankrupt's estate.

[in the event of a person named in paragraph 1 withdrawing or being eliminated from any vote for the appointment of a liquidator/trustee the proxy-holder may vote or abstain in any further ballot at his/her discretion]

Any other resolutions which the proxy-holder is to propose or vote in favour of or against should be set out in numbered paragraphs in the space provided below paragraph 1. If more room is required please use the other side of this form.

_____
_____
_____
_____
_____
_____
_____
_____
_____
_____
_____
_____
_____
_____

This form must be signed

Signature _____ **Date** _____

Name in CAPITAL LETTERS _____

Only to be completed if the creditor/ contributory has not signed in person

Position with creditor/contributory or relationship to creditor/contributory or other authority for signature _____

_____
_____

Remember: there may be resolutions on the other side of this form.

Form 36 Proof of debt—general form

(see p 52 Prescribed Form 4.25)

(TITLE)

Date of Winding-Up Order/Resolution for voluntary winding-up

1	Name of Creditor	
2	Address of Creditor	
3	Total amount of claim, including any Value Added Tax and outstanding uncapitalised interest as at the date the company went into liquidation [see Note]	£
4	Details of any document by reference to which the debt can be substantiated. [Note: the liquidator may call for any document or evidence to substantiate the claim at his discretion]	
5	If the total amount shown above includes Value Added Tax, please show:— (a) amount of Value Added Tax (b) amount of claim NET of Value Added Tax	 £ £
6	If total amount above includes outstanding uncapitalised interest please state amount	£
7	If you have filled in both box 3 and box 5, please state whether you are claiming the amount shown in box 3 or the amount shown in box 5(b)	
8	Give details of whether the whole or any part of the debt falls within any (and if so which) of the categories of preferential debts under section 386 of, and schedule 6 to, the Insolvency Act 1986 (as read with schedule 3 to the Social Security Pensions Act 1975)	Category Amount(s) claimed as preferential £

9	Particulars of how and when debt incurred	
10	Particulars of any security held, the value of the security, and the date it was given	£

11 Signature of creditor or person authorised to act on his behalf _____

Name in BLOCK LETTERS _____

Position with or relation to creditor _____

Admitted to vote for

£

Date

Liquidator

Admitted preferentially for

£

Date

Liquidator

Admitted non-preferentially for

£

Date

Liquidator

NOTE: A company goes into liquidation if it passes a resolution for voluntary winding up or an order for its winding up is made by the court at a time when it has not already gone into liquidation by passing such a resolution.

Form 37 Affidavit of debt
(*see p 52 Prescribed Form 4.26*)

(TITLE)

(a) Insert full name, address and description of person making oath

I (a)

make oath and say:—

(b) Delete as applicable

(c) State capacity eg director, secretary, solicitor etc

(d) State full name and address of creditor

(e) State means of knowledge of matters sworn to in affidavit

(1) That (b) [I am a creditor of the above named company [I am (c)

of (d)

a creditor of the above named company.
I have been concerned in this matter (e)

and am authorised by
the creditor to make this affidavit on its/his behalf]

(f) Insert date

(2) That the said company on (f)   the date on which the company
went into liquidation* was and still is justly and truly indebted (b) [to me] [to the
said creditor] in the sum of £   as shown in the proof of debt exhibited
hereto marked "A".

Sworn at

*NOTE: A company goes into liquidation if it passes a resolution for voluntary
winding up or an order for its winding up is made by the court at a time
when it has not already gone into liquidation by passing such a
resolution.

Form 38 Rejection of proof
(*see p 56*)

(*Title as in Form 2*)

TAKE NOTICE that, as [Official Receiver and] Liquidator of the above named company, I have this day rejected your claim against the company (*if proof wholly rejected strike out following words* [to the extent of £   ] on the following grounds;

Either

That in spite of repeated requests you have neglected to produce evidence in support of your claim.

Or

That your claim represents the invoice price of work done for the company in an unsatisfactory and incomplete manner as a result of which the company had to have the work re-done and completed by another contractor.

Or

That your claim is barred by the provision of the Limitation Act 1980.

Or

(*as the case may be*)

AND FURTHER TAKE NOTICE that subject to the power of the court to extend the time, no application to reverse or vary my decision in rejecting your Proof will be entertained after the expiration of 21 days from this date.

Dated this   day of   199

. . . .

[Official Receiver and] Liquidator

To   of (*address*)

**Form 39   Summons or notice of motion to reverse or vary
liquidator's decision on proof**
(*see p 56*)

(*Title as in Form 2*)

LET L.L. of (*address*) attend [*or in courts other than the High Court*
TAKE NOTICE that this court will be moved] (*continue with formal
parts as in Form 16*) on the hearing of an application by A.B. of
(*address*), [claiming to be] a creditor [*or* contributory] of the above
named company, for an order that the decision of the Respondent,
the [Official Receiver and] Liquidator of the abovenamed company.

Either

in rejecting the Proof of the Applicant A.B. in the above matters
for the sum of £   may be reversed and the said Proof may be
ordered to be admitted in full.

Or

in rejecting the Proof of the Applicant A.B. in the above matters
for the sum of £   to the extent of £   may be varied and that
the said Proof may be Ordered to be admitted [in full *or* for the
further sum of £   ]

Or

in admitting the Proof of J.K. in the above matters may be reversed
and the said Proof Ordered to be rejected [in full *or* as to £   ]
AND that the said [Official Receiver and] Liquidator may be
Ordered to pay the costs of and incidental to this application.
(*Conclude as in Form 16*)

[Adapted by kind permission of Butterworth & Co (Publishers) Ltd
from Atkin's Court Forms Vol 10 (1981 Issue), title Companies—
Winding Up Form 270]

Form 40   Affidavit in support of summons to reverse liquidator's decision on proof
(*see p 56*)

(Title as in Form 2)

I, A.B. of (*residence and description*), make oath and say as follows;
1. The abovenamed company was ordered to be wound up on the   day of   199 and by an Order dated the   day of   199 L.L. was appointed liquidator thereof.
2. On   day of   199 , I lodged with the Liquidator a Proof for the sum of £   in respect of goods sold and delivered, particulars of which were annexed to the said Proof, a copy of which, together with the said particulars, is now produced and shown to me marked 'AB1'.
3. On   day of   199 , I received a notice of rejection of the said Proof from the Liquidator, a copy of which is now produced and shown to me marked 'AB2', which states as the ground of rejection that (*specify the ground as in Form 38*).
4. (*State the applicant's answer to the liquidator's contention*).
Sworn

[Adapted by kind permission of Butterworth & Co (Publishers) Ltd from Atkin's Court Forms Vol 10 (1981 Issue), title Companies— Winding Up Form 271]

Form 41 Order reversing or varying rejection of proof or giving leave to amend proof
(*see p 56*)

(*Title as in Form 2*)

UPON THE APPLICATION by summons dated   199   of A.B. of (*address*) [*or* UPON MOTION this day made unto this court by Counsel on behalf of A.B.]
AND UPON HEARING Counsel for the Applicant and for L.L. the liquidator of the abovenamed company (the Respondent)
AND UPON HEARING the order to wind up the said company dated   199 , the order dated   199   (appointing liquidator) the Proof of Debt of the Applicant filed   199   the Notice dated   199   by the Respondent as such Liquidator rejecting the said Proof of Debt the Affidavit of A.B. filed   199 and the exhibit in the said affidavit referred to
IT IS ORDERED that the decision of the Respondent as such liquidator rejecting the said Proof of Debt of the Applicant [for the sum *or* to the extent] of £   be [reversed *or* varied] and that such Proof be admitted in the winding up of the said company for the [said] sum of £

Or

IT IS ORDERED that the Applicant be at liberty to amend his said Proof of Debt so as to prove in the winding up of the said company as a creditor for the sum of £
AND IT IS ORDERED that the Respondent as such liquidator do admit the said Proof as so amended to rank for dividend in the winding up of the said company for the said sum of £

Then

AND IT IS ORDERED that the costs of the Applicant A.B. of the said application be taxed (if not agreed) and paid out of the assets of the said company.

[Adapted by kind permission of Butterworth & Co (Publishers) Ltd from Atkin's Court Forms Vol 10 (1981 Issue), title Companies— Winding Up Forms 272 & 276]

Form 42 **Authority to liquidator to pay dividends to another person**
(*see p 58*)

(*Title as in Form 2*)

To the [Official Receiver and] Liquidator

Sir,

I/We hereby authorise and request you to pay to F.G. of (*address*) (a specimen of whose signature is given below), all dividends as they are declared in the abovenamed matter, and which may become due and payable to me/us in respect of the Proof of Debt for the sum of £ against the abovenamed company, made by on my/our behalf.

And I/we further request that the cheque or cheques drawn in respect of such dividends may be made payable to the order of the said F.G. whose receipt shall be sufficient authority to you for the issue of such cheque or cheques in his name. It is understood that this authority is to remain in force until revoked by me/us in writing.

. . . . (*signature*)

Witness to the signature of creditor . . . .

Dated this   day of   199

. . . . (*specimen of the signature of* F.G. *appointed as above*)

[Adapted by kind permission of Butterworth & Co (Publishers) Ltd from Atkin's Court Forms Vol 10 (1981 Issue), title Companies—Winding Up Form 296]

Form 43 VAT Bad Debt Relief Form
(see p 57)

XYZ LIMITED—IN LIQUIDATION

(Resolution to wind up— .... 199)

or   (Date of winding up order— .... 199)

Name and address of creditor ....

....

....

....

Amount of claim submitted £ ....

(Amount in words) ....

....

£	Amount excluding VAT
£	VAT
£	Total

As requested I confirm that the above claim has been submitted to myself as liquidator of the above company.

.... (signature of liquidator)

(Note—this acknowledgement is for use in connection with VAT Bad Debt Relief and does not confer any rights as a Creditor.)

Form 44 Petitioner's bill of costs of a petition to wind up
(*see p 38*)

(*Title as in Form 2*)

Petitioner's bill of costs of a petition to wind up to be taxed pursuant to order dated   199   on a party and party basis and paid out of the assets of the company.

VAT Registration Number (*of solicitors*)

Taxed Off		Value Added Tax	Disbursements	Profit Costs
	1(b) Preparing presenting and issuing of petition			Discretionary
	— Paid fee on issue	—	40.00	
	Paid deposit to Official Receiver	—	240.00	
	3(c) Preparing affidavit verifying petition (per page (unless more than 5, then £1 per page))			3.00
	— Paid oath fee (including exhibit)	—	4.50	
	— Paid agent's fee for service of petition on company			
	3(c) Preparing affidavit of service, engrossing, attending deponent to swear and filing			3.00
	— Paid oath fee (including exhibit)	—	4.50	
	3(b) Preparing advertisement (per page)			
	— Paid fee for London Gazette	—	12.50	
	2 Preparing, issuing, filing and service on company of summons for appointment of provisional liquidator (£2–£14)			
	3(c) Preparing affidavit in support (per page)			3.00
	Paid oath fee	—	3.50	
	6 Attending before registrar when order made (£2–£17)			
	3(d) Brief to counsel on hearing of petition (per page)			3.00
	Copies of documents for counsel (per A4 page, if photocopied)			0.15
	— Paid counsel's fee on brief and conference			
	7 Attending appointing and on conference with counsel			4.00
	8 Attending hearing when order for winding up made and costs to be taxed and paid out of the company's assets (£5–£21)			

Taxed Off		Value Added Tax	Disbursements	Profit Costs
	Attending lodging documents and for order			
10	Preparation for hearing;			
	The matter was handled throughout by a partner/solicitor/managing clerk/legal executive.			
	Expense rate £ per hour.			
	Untimed telephone calls charged at £ each.			
	Letters written charged £ each and letters received charged £ each.			
	Part A—Work Done			
	Petitioning Creditor;			
	Correspondence with and attendances upon the petitioning creditor obtaining instructions to petition and to inform him of progress. Obtaining instructions to apply for the appointment of a provisional liquidator and obtaining detailed evidence in support of such application.			
	Attendances—(number) lasting a total of hours			
	telephone calls			
	letters written			
	letters received			
	Witnesses;			
	(set out details similar to above)			
	Searches;			
	Correspondence with company agents obtaining details of the company from the official file.			
	letters written			
	letters received			
	Paid search fee			
	Service;			
	Correspondence with enquiry agents as to service of the petition on the company			
	letters written			
	letters received			
	Documents;			
	Referring to the file from time to time and perusing and considering all necessary documents; also collating all necessary documents			

Taxed Off	Value Added Tax	Disburse- ments	Profit Costs
and evidence preparatory to drawing brief to counsel Engaged hours TOTAL PART A—£ Part B—Care and Conduct Charged at % TOTAL PART B—£ TOTAL Preparation Item 12(a) Taxation of costs including preparation of bill and copies, collating documents to accompany, lodging, attending on taxation and completing same Engaged hours			
Total			
Less taxed off			
Add disbursements			
Add VAT on profit costs Add VAT on disbursements			
Add taxing fee			
Total			

We certify that the castings of this
bill are correct

. . . .
(solicitors for the petitioning
creditor)

I certify that I have taxed and
allowed the within bill of costs on
a party and party basis in the sum
of £   including £   VAT.
Dated this   day of
199 .

. . . .
(District Judge/Taxing Officer)

Note: VAT should not be claimed if the petitioning creditor is VAT
registered.

Form 45   Company's bill of costs of petition to wind up
        (*see p 38*)

(*Title as in Form 2*)

Company's Bill of Costs of opposing petition to wind up to be taxed pursuant to order dated   199 on a party and party basis and paid by the petitioner

VAT Registration Number (*of solicitors*)

Taxed Off		Value Added Tax	Disburse-ments	Profit Costs
	Paid for copy affidavit verifying the petition (per page)		0.25	
3(c)	Preparing affidavit in answer (per page)			3.00
—	Paid oath fee	—	2.00	
6	Attending hearing of application for appointment of provisional liquidator (£2–£17)			
3(d)	Brief to counsel on hearing of the petition (per page)			3.00
	(*and then continue as in Form 44*)			

Form 46   Creditor's bill of or contributory's costs of petition to wind up
(*see p 38*)

(*Title as in Form 2*)

Creditor's (or contributory's) costs of opposing/supporting petition to wind up to be taxed pursuant to order dated   199 on a party and party basis and paid by the petitioner/out of assets of the company

VAT Registration Number (*of solicitors*)

Taxed Off		Value Added Tax	Disburse-ments	Profit Costs
—	Paid for copy petition (per page)		0.25	
3(b)	Notice of intention to appear			3.00
3(d)	Brief to counsel on hearing of petition (per page)			
	(*and then continue as in Form 44*)			3.00

Index

Adjournment, 34–5
Administration—
  winding up proceedings, effect on, 20–2
Administrative order, 20
  discharge, winding up after, 109
Advertisement, 17–18, 93–6
Appeals, 40–1

Balance sheet test, 8

Cash flow test, 8
Company—
  proceedings against, 22, 42
Contributories, 10
  meetings, *see* Meetings
  petition, 14, 86–1
    cost of, 128
Copy petitions, 18
Costs—
  company's, 127
  creditor's or contributory's, 128
  of hearing, 36–8, 110
  petitioner's, 124–6
County courts, jurisdiction, 3
Creditors—
  meetings, *see* Meetings
  petition, 14
    after statutory demand, 81
    costs, 128
    inability to pay debts, 83
    levying execution, 82
    on simple debt, 80
    substitution of, 28–9, 104
  rights of, 65–7
  secured, 57–8
  wishes of, in respect of order, 35

Debts—
  affidavit of, 52, 117
  bills of exchange, 54
  disputed, 7–8
  interest on, 56–7
  payable in future, 54
  promissory notes, 54
  provable, 53
  secured creditors, 57–8
  VAT, 57, 123
  see also Creditors; Proof of debts
Dispositions, 27
Disputed debts, 7–8
Dividends, proof of, 58–9
  assignment of, 58, 122

Equitable grounds, *see* Just and
    equitable grounds
Execution, 22–3, 82

Fees—
  Court, 2

General title form, 75
Grounds—
  inability to pay, 6–10, 83
  just and equitable, 10–12, 84

Hearing—
  adjournment, 34–5
  appeals, 40–1
  costs, 36–8, 110
  powers of court, 33
  winding up order, 39, 108
    rescission of, 39–40
    whether should be made, 35–6
  see also Preliminary hearing

Hearing—*contd*
High Court jurisdiction, 2–3

Inability to pay, 6–10, 83
  statutory demand form, 8, 72–4
Insolvency, 8
Interest on debts, 50–7
Interlocutory matters—
  dispositions, avoidance of, 27
  execution, 22–3, 82
  provisional liquidator, 23–6, 97–8
  restraint powers, 20–2, 95–6
  special manager appointment, 23,
    102

Jurisdiction, 1–5
  concurrent, 4
  county courts, 3
  High Court, 2–3
  open court, and chambers, 4–5
  transfer between courts, 3
Just and equitable grounds, 10–12
  petition form, 84

Liquidation, voluntary, *see* Voluntary
    liquidation
Liquidation committee—
  dealings with members, 63
  expenses of members, 64
  functions and rights of, 61–2
  meetings of, 62
  membership and establishment, 60
  resolutions by post, 62
  termination of membership, 63
  vacancies, 63
  where no committee, 64
Liquidator—
  appointment at first meeting, 48–9
    certification of, 49
  powers exercised with sanction, 61
  provisional, *see* Provisional
    Liquidator removal of, 51
  resignation, and vacancies, 50

Meetings—
  business at first, 48–9
  liquidation committee, 62
  liquidator, appointment, 49–50
  notice of first, 44, 111–12
  proxies, 46–8
  removal of liquidator, 51
  rules governing, 44–6

Official receiver—
  certification of liquidator, 49
  duties after orders, 43–4
  notice of meetings, 44
  provisional liquidation and, 24–6, 42
  reports to creditors, 66–7
Opposition, 32

Petition—
  administration provisions, effect of,
    20–2
  advertisement of, 17–18, 93–6
    as notice, 18
  affidavits in opposition, 32
  contributories, 14, 86, 128
  copy, 18
  costs, 124–8
  creditor, *see* Creditors
  endorsement, 15
  execution and, 22–3, 82
  forms, general 76–8
  irregularities, 19
  issue of, 15
  just and equitable, 84
  order dismissing, 33, 110
  resolution by company, 79
  service of, 15–16, 90–2
  verification of, 17, 88–9
  when voluntarily wound up, 85
  withdrawal of, 28–9, 103
Petitioners, 13
  substitution, 29–30, 104
  see also Creditors; Contributories
Preliminary hearing—
  affidavits in opposition, 32
  compliance with rules, 30–1, 105
  persons intending to appear—
    list of, 31, 107
    notice by, 31–2, 106
  substitution of petitioners, 29–30,
    104
  withdrawal of petition, 28–9, 103
Proof of debts—
  admission and rejection of, 55–6,
    118
  alteration of, 56, 119–21
  contents of, 53
  forms of, 52, 115–16
  time for, 54–5
  see also Debts
Provisional liquidator—
  additional powers, 26, 100

Petition—*contd*
  after order, 42
  appointment, 23–6, 97–8
  consent to act, 101
Proxies—
  forms of, 47, 113–14
  lodging of, 47
  need for, 46
  solicitation for, 47–8
  voting by, 48

Rescission of order, 39–40
Restraint powers, 20–2, 95–6
Rules of the Supreme Court—
  winding up proceedings, applying
    to, 1–2

Service of petition, 15–16
  proved by affidavit, 16, 90–2
Special manager, 23, 102
Statement of affairs—
  notice requiring, 99
Statutory demand, 8, 19, 72–4
Substitution, 29–30, 104

Unregistered companies—
  winding up, 2

Value added tax, 57, 123
Verification of petition, 17, 88–9
Voluntary liquidation, 9
  petition form when in, 85
  winding up order and, 9, 36

Winding up—
  interlocutory matters, 20–6
  matters arising after, 42–51
  preliminary hearing, 28–32
  restraint of, 20–2, 195–6
  see also Grounds; Petition; Winding
    up order
Winding up order, 39, 108
  following administrative order
    discharge, 109
  rescission of, 39–40
  voluntary liquidation and, 9, 36
  wishes of creditors, 35
  see also Hearing